SOPHOCLES

THE THEBAN PLAYS

OEDIPUS THE KING, the most famous of these three famous plays, has been characterized by critics from Aristotle to Coleridge as the perfect exemplar of the art of tragedy. The other two, OEDIPUS AT COLONUS, in which the blind king finds his final release from the sufferings the gods have brought upon him, and ANTIGONE, which completes the downfall of the House of Cadmus through the actions of Oedipus' magnificent and uncompromising daughter, are equally distinguished. The three together represent Attic drama at the pitch of its achievement.

EVERYMAN,
I WILL GO WITH THEE,
AND BE THY GUIDE,
IN THY MOST NEED
TO GO BY THY SIDE

SOPHOCLES

The Theban Plays

OEDIPUS THE KING
OEDIPUS AT COLONUS
ANTIGONE

Translated by David Grene
with an Introduction by Charles Segal
and Notes by James Hogan
General Editors – David Grene and
Richmond Lattimore

E V E R Y M A N ' S L I B R A R Y

Alfred A. Knopf New York Toronto

93

THIS IS A BORZOI BOOK

PUBLISHED BY ALFRED A. KNOPF, INC.

First included in Everyman's Library, 1906
This translation first published in Everyman's Library, 1994

Licensed by the University of Chicago Press, Chicago, Illinois
© 1991 by The University of Chicago. All right reserved.
Sophocles: Oedipus the King
© 1942 by The University of Chicago
Sophocles: Oedipus at Colonus
© 1991 by The University of Chicago
Sophocles: Antigone
© 1991 by The University of Chicago

Introduction, Bibliography, Chronology and Notes Copyright
© 1994 by David Campbell Publishers Ltd.
Typography by Peter B. Willberg

All rights reserved under International and Pan-American Copyright
Conventions. Published in the United States by Alfred A. Knopf,
Inc., New York, and simultaneously in Canada by Random House
of Canada Limited, Toronto. Distributed by Random House, Inc.,
New York

ISBN 0-679-43132-2
LC 94-5984

Library of Congress Cataloging-in-Publication Data
Sophocles.
The Theban plays / Sophocles.
p.   cm.—(Everyman's library (Alfred A. Knopf))
ISBN 0-679-43132-2: $17.00
1. Sophocles—Translations into English. 2. Greek drama (Tragedy)
—Translations into English. 3. Antigone (Greek mythology)—
Drama. 4. Oedipus (Greek mythology)—Drama. I. Title.
PA4414.A2   1994   94-5984
882'.01—dc20   CIP

Book Design by Barbara de Wilde and Carol Devine Carson

Typeset in the UK by MS Filmsetting Ltd., Frome, Somerset

Printed and bound in Germany by
Mohndruck Graphische Betriebe GmbH, Gütersloh

THE THEBAN PLAYS

C O N T E N T S

INTRODUCTION

THE POET

'Happy Sophocles, who lived a long life and died a happy man, a man of skill. He died well, having fashioned many beautiful tragedies, enduring no suffering.' These lines might seem a strange way to describe a tragedian, but the comic poet Phrynichus wrote them about Sophocles (497–406 BC) the year after his death.[1] For all the conflict, suffering, and pessimism in the plays, the life of their creator seems to have been indeed fortunate. Born into a wealthy family in the area of Athens known as Colonus, the site of his last play, Sophocles held positions of honor and importance in his city during its greatest period and remained a respected and apparently admired figure in both public and private.

Unlike his older rival, Aeschylus (525–456 BC), and his younger contemporary, Euripides (485–406 BC), Sophocles never exiled himself from Athens. He served as state supervisor of the tribute of the Athenian empire in 443–442, as general with Pericles in the revolt of Samos in 441–440, and in his old age as one of the ten Probouloi or commissioners in charge of the conservative Council of Five Hundred after the oligarchic coup of 411. He was also a priest of a minor healing divinity called Alkon and on one occasion, according to the ancient *Life of Sophocles*, received the sacred snake of the healing god Asclepius into his house. A later source reports that he was awarded cultic honors after his death for this service, under the title Dexion, 'the Receiver'.

Given the fact that ancient worship emphasized cultic performance rather than belief in dogma, such activities do not exclude a spirit of inquiry and openness about the gods. Thus Sophocles could also be a member of the advanced intellectual circles around Pericles, which included speculative philosophers like Anaxagoras, travelling lecturers and teachers of rhetoric like the Sophist Protagoras, the ethnographer-historian Herodotus, and the artist Pheidias, the sculptor of the Parthenon. Nevertheless, his activity in these local cults is certainly consistent with the deep interest in the gods that his plays exhibit, while his active political life is also consistent with the plays' concern with the nature of civic authority and conflicts within the city. To complete the possible congruences of man and work, the biographical tradition reports an active and varied sex life, so that personal experience and interest may lie behind the powerful ode on love in *Antigone* and the theme of sexual desire and jealousy in the *Trachinian Women*.

Sophocles was fortunate not only in the circumstances of his life but also in his time. He was old enough to have experienced his city's surge of confidence when Athens and her allies defeated the invading Persians in 480–478; and he is said to have danced in the chorus of young men celebrating the naval victory of Salamis in 480. The years of his maturity were Athens' greatest period. Guided by its ambitious and patriotic leader Pericles, the city-state developed its hegemony after the Persian victory into a maritime empire that dominated the eastern Aegean. The tribute paid by the subject allies maintained the strong Athenian navy as a defense against the continuing threat of Persia but also financed the city's cultural and political institutions. The monumental public buildings of Periclean Athens are still to be admired today: the impressive entrance to the Acropolis known as the Propylaea, the massive and graceful temple of Athena called the Parthenon, whose famous sculptures were executed by Pheidias, the elegant smaller temple of Athena Nike, the Erechtheum, with its famous caryatids, and the great temple of Athena and Hephaestus known as the Theseion dominating the Agora or Marketplace. Pericles' vision was of an Athens that embodied the highest possible achievements in the arts and sciences of the time, and it is set forth in the Funeral Speech that Thucydides has him speak in his *History of the Peloponnesian War*, where he calls Athens 'the education of Greece' (2.41.1). Conflicts with the other city-states of Greece, however, led by Sparta and Corinth caused the outbreak of the Peloponnesian War in 431 BC. Lasting nearly thirty years, it eventually sapped Athens' energies. Pericles himself died in a plague in the second year of the war (429 BC), and Athens finally capitulated to Sparta and its allies in 404.

INTRODUCTION

As part of his cultural program, Pericles built a music hall or Odeion and also refurbished the stone theater of Dionysus nearby, on the southern slope of the Acropolis, where three tragic poets were chosen each year to perform their plays at the festival of Dionysus. Sophocles won eighteen first-place victories in these annual competitions, achieving his first victory over Aeschylus in 468 BC. The tradition lists 123 plays, of which only seven have survived: the three Theban plays, plus *Ajax* (460–450 BC), *Trachinian Women* (440–430?), *Electra* (420–410?), and *Philoctetes* (409). There are extensive fragments of a satyr-drama, *The Trackers* (*Ichneutae*), recovered from papyri preserved in the sands of Egypt, and numerous brief quotations from the lost plays preserved mostly by later writers.

THE THEBAN PLAYS

Although the *Antigone*, *Oedipus Tyrannus* (*Oedipus the King* in this translation), and *Oedipus at Colonus* are often grouped together as the 'Theban Plays', they are not a trilogy in the way that the three plays of Aeschylus' *Oresteia* form a trilogy. Sophocles' three dramas about the house of Oedipus, king of Thebes, were written at three widely spaced intervals: *Antigone* probably in 442–441 BC, *Oedipus Tyrannus* probably between 429 and 425 BC, and *Oedipus at Colonus* in the last years of the poet's life. This last was presented posthumously by his grandson (also named Sophocles) in 402–401 BC. The date of *Antigone* depends on the anecdote that its popularity helped Sophocles' election to the generalship in the following year. The date of the *Tyrannus* rests mainly on the assumed connection between the plague that broke out in Athens during this period, itself a consequence of the massing of the population behind the city's walls because of the war.

Despite the fact that Sophocles wrote these three plays at different times, there are many connections and verbal echoes between them, but also major differences. Each of the three plays, for example, offers a different version of the succession at Thebes after Oedipus' self-blinding. Yet the last play, the *Coloneus*, clearly resumes the questions of guilt and responsibility raised in the *Tyrannus* some twenty years earlier. Sophocles also seems to have maintained and developed his conception of some of the main characters over many years. Oedipus' affection for his daughters at the end of the *Tyrannus* continues in the later play, while the fierce anger that he displays to Creon and Teiresias in the *Tyrannus*, when he thinks that they have betrayed him, is consistent with his unforgiving harshness to the sons who have driven him from Thebes in the *Coloneus*. Antigone, the devoted daughter who accompanies her father into exile and then resolves to go back to Thebes to help her brothers at the end of the *Coloneus*, is a plausibly younger and softer version of the Antigone who is so involved with family in the play named after her. The tyrannical, authoritarian Creon of this play, who intimidates the elders of Thebes, is consistent with the determined, self-righteous, and violent Creon of the *Coloneus*.

THE MYTH

Greek tragedy marks an important step in the increasingly ethical and philosophical interpretation of the ancient myths that runs from Homer and Hesiod on to Plato and the allegorizers of later antiquity. The Greek poets told and retold these myths with inventiveness, imagination, and powerful, expressive images, each in his own way. They used these tales to probe the depths of human nature and thereby shaped a body of material into which were distilled the reflection and experience of centuries.

The tragedians of the fifth century generally drew their material from the great storehouse of myth and legend that they inherited from the bards and singers who composed from the eighth to the sixth centuries BC. Of these songs and poems only a small portion now survives, in which Homer's *Iliad* and *Odyssey* are especially important. These myths, in turn, probably reflect tales told or sung in the great period of Mycenaean civilization many centuries before. The protagonists of these myths are generally the rather shadowy kings and queens of these remote times (approximately from 1500 to 1100 BC), whose palaces are still to be seen in the massive ruins of Mycenae, Tiryns, and Pylos.

Thebes was one such Mycenaean kingdom, supposedly founded by Cadmus from Phoenicia, who populated it by sowing in the earth the teeth of the serpent that he killed on its site (hence the term 'Sown Men' or Spartoi for the Thebans). Cadmus' descendant, the Theban king Laius, son of Labdacus, receives an oracle not to beget a son, does so (in some versions in drunkenness), exposes the child (Oedipus), who later accidentally kills Laius, marries Laius' queen and his own mother, Jocasta, and becomes king. This portion of the myth is told in the *Oedipus Tyrannus*.

Many versions of the Theban myth were told from the eighth to the fifth century BC. The earliest reference, in *Iliad* 23.679–80, seems to imply Oedipus' death in battle and burial at Thebes, a version that excludes the self-blinding of the *Tyrannus*. The *Odyssey* refers to Jocasta's suicide by hanging but makes no mention of the oracles, Oedipus' self-blinding, or the children (11.271–80). Yet the story already has its tragic tone: Oedipus continues to rule in Thebes 'suffering woes through the destructive counsels of the gods'; and Jocasta, in dying, 'left behind for him all those many woes that the Furies of a mother accomplish'. Another early epic version, a poem known as the *Oedipodeia*, now lost, mitigated the incestuous marriage by attributing the children to a second wife, called Euryganeia. One of the most interesting early versions has recently been recovered from a papyrus fragment of a poem by Stesichorus (early sixth century BC).[2] It contains a speech, probably by Jocasta, in which she pleads with the prophet Teiresias to keep her two sons from killing one another in civil war; and she proposes a division of the kingdom and the property between them. The existence of this poem shows, among other things, that Sophocles had a literary model for the development of Jocasta's character in the *Tyrannus*.

In the generation before the *Antigone* and *Oedipus Tyrannus*, Sophocles' great predecessor, Aeschylus, had dramatized the story in a trilogy, *Laius*, *Oedipus*, *Seven against Thebes*, and a satyr-play, *Sphinx* (467 BC). This work was doubtless the most important single influence on Sophocles; but unfortunately only the last play of the trilogy, the *Seven*, survives. From that play and from a few surviving fragments, however, we can reconstruct Aeschylus' interpretation of the legend. He viewed the tragedy of Oedipus as the result of the family curse that spreads over several generations. In the first play Laius is cursed by Pelops for raping his son, Chrysippus, and thus causing his death. Laius begets his son, Oedipus, in defiance of an oracle from Apollo that tells him three times not to sire a child or else he will destroy his city.

Aeschylus' *Oedipus* seems to have resembled the Sophoclean play in general outline, but Aeschylus located the deadly meeting between father and son near a shrine of the Furies in southern Boeotia, not at the crossroads between Delphi and Thebes. Sophocles changed the site probably to avoid the heavy Aeschylean emphasis on the family curse (which the Furies bring to fulfillment) and to stress the motifs of prophecy and Oedipus' self-discovery and self-knowledge, which are connected with Delphi and its oracle of Apollo. The climax of the Aeschylean play seems to have been Oedipus' self-blinding, as in Sophocles; and indeed this is the first time that this motif is attested in the myth. The last play, *The Seven against Thebes*, describes Polyneices' attack upon his city and the death of the two brothers at one another's hands.

Aeschylus did not invent the tradition of the family curse, however, for his contemporary, the Theban poet Pindar (*c.* 522–438 BC), writing about a decade before the *Seven*, alluded to it, taking up the motif of the Fury or Erinys from the *Odyssey* (*Olympian Odes*, 2.38–42). Because Sophocles treats the myth in three separate plays and not in a connected trilogy, he viewed the story in terms of the choices, personalities, and emotions of his individual protagonists. The *Tyrannus* completely suppresses the Furies; the *Antigone* consigns them and the family curse to the background; and the *Coloneus* transforms the Furies into the awesome but ultimately kindly Eumenides, who receive Oedipus into their sacred grove. The oracle to Laius in the *Tyrannus* has the form of a mere statement of fact (the child will kill his father) rather than a direct prohibition as in Aeschylus (to save the city, die without begetting offspring, *Seven against Thebes*, 748–9). Sophocles is more interested in how Oedipus pieces together the isolated fragments of his past to discover who and what he is and in tracing the hero's response to this new vision of himself. He thus replaces Oedipus' terrible curse on the sons that may have ended Aeschylus' *Oedipus* with the remarkably tender scene of concern for his daughters, with very little said of the sons. Indeed, this dismissal of the sons may have been Sophocles' way of signalling to the connoisseurs in the audience how much he has innovated upon the familiar Aeschylean version (*OT*, 1459–61).

ANTIGONE

Since Hegel's celebrated discussion of this play in his *Philosophy of Fine Art* (1823–7), interpreters have often taken its central theme to be a conflict between state and individual in which each has a claim to justice. Such an approach may be an interesting philosophical extrapolation but is not faithful to Sophocles' intentions. Creon may be the ruler of Thebes, but he does not embody the state in any absolute sense, as his son Haemon warns, and he becomes increasingly obsessed with his personal authority as the play continues. Antigone does not sacrifice her life for an abstract notion of individual rights but to perform the family's obligatory funerary rites for blood kin and to honor the chthonic deities, those who look after the dead in the Underworld (450–70:494–514).

Alongside her spiritual strength, courage, and integrity moreover, Antigone has a fierceness and single-minded determination that remind the chorus of the 'savage spirit' of her father, Oedipus (471:515). Her devotion to her dead brother is matched by her severity toward her sister, Ismene, who tells her, 'You have a warm heart for such chilly deeds' (88:102). Ismene is the foil to Antigone and embodies the warmer, gentler, more feminine side of herself that Antigone rejects. It is Ismene who recalls the betrothal between Antigone and Haemon that Creon had callously dismissed (571–2:629–30):

Creon: I hate a bad wife for a son of mine.
Antigone: Dear Haemon, how your father dishonors you.[3]

In the opening scene Ismene's failure of nerve in the defiance that Antigone proposes to her sets the stage for her sister's tragic isolation. At the end of Aeschylus' *Seven against Thebes* the chorus of Theban women is divided, and half of them would join Antigone in burying her brother.[4] In Sophocles,

Antigone has no allies; for most of the play she stands entirely alone, a bitter paradox for one whose devotion is to the family.

The dominant forces in this play are death and love, but they operate in the larger frame of the polis (city-state) and its civic religion and familial funerary cult and not just in individual lives. Antigone is, as she says, a Bride of Hades (810–16:873–7), a term used of young women who die before marriage.[5] Having committed herself to burial rites for her brother, she, a young girl engaged to be married, will win heroic honor, like a man, by lying in death beside her dear brother in the paradoxical 'holy wrongdoing' of her innocent crime (71–7:79–89).

By choosing a young girl as the opponent of the Theban king, Sophocles emphasizes the paradox that these religious sanctions, though defended by no visible human power, cannot be violated with impunity. Creon, in his definition of civic life as narrowly political, learns too late from Teiresias' prophecies that he has tampered with laws that extend far beyond the 'decrees' that he can issue to the citizens of Thebes.

In a terrible symmetry Antigone, 'lying with the dead Polyneices below' (71:83–4), is answered by Haemon lying beside Antigone in her cave of death, figuratively consummating a union in death, a marriage in Hades (1234–41:1311–19). The punishment for interfering with the dead is that the young, marriageable people who should continue the life of their respective houses are turned into corpses. The inversions of life and death receive a powerful stage enactment as Creon returns to the stage in the last scene bearing in his arms his dead son Haemon. In his crazed attack upon his father at the mouth of the cave, Haemon re-enacts Oedipus' crime against his father. When Creon's wife, Eurydice, exits in silence, like Jocasta, to commit suicide inside the palace, his house becomes a mirror-image of Oedipus' house. It is as if the curse of Oedipus, of which the chorus sings in the third ode, has migrated from Antigone's house to Creon's.

As in the story of Oedipus too, the sufferings of Thebes become increasingly intertwined with the sufferings in the house of the king. The inversions of upper and lower worlds and the juxtapositions of Olympian and chthonic religion join the areas of family and city in exploring the larger theme of man's relation with nature and the gods. The choral odes in particular gradually expand the frame of reference from Thebes and its defensive walls and temples in the first ode to remote Thrace in later odes and to Dionysus, invoked as the healing cleanser of Thebes' pollutions in the last ode (1140–45:1215-18). His nocturnal rituals of maenads, as the chorus sings, make him 'leader in the dance of the fire-pulsing stars,/ master of the voices of night' (1146–51:1219–25). The fiery stars and the purifying god who leaps joyfully over mountaintops, however, only set off the enclosure or darkness in which the human sufferers die: Antigone and Haemon in the underground cave, Eurydice at the altar inside the palace, Creon re-entering his house, which he calls a 'harbor of Hades' that cannot receive the purification for which the chorus invoked Dionysus (1284:1361, 'haven of death').

The second and third odes (332–83 and 582–630:368–411 and 640–78) articulate contrasting positions on man's place in the world. The former passage, known as the Ode on Man, is one of the most famous odes of Greek tragedy. Listing humanity's achievements in subduing nature, it recalls Prometheus' list of the achievements of civilization in Aeschylus' *Prometheus Bound*. But Sophocles' praise of man also warns about the one thing that he has not subdued, namely Hades, the realm of death, which, as we have seen, comes to dominate the action (360–62:396–7). The ode's opening words call man 'something wondrous', *deinon*, but the word also means 'a thing of terror', and the passage echoes a celebrated ode in Aeschylus' *Libation Bearers* (585ff.) on the monstrosities nurtured by earth and sea, of which none are more terrible than the daring will and devices of desperate men and women.

The subsequent ode sings of the terrible curse on the house of Oedipus in images of the dark, turbulent sea, not the controlled sea of the Ode on Man, and blood, murder, and madness. Taken together, the two odes set out the extreme limits of man's potential relation to his world: his domination of the environment by reason and technology on the one hand and his subjection to mysterious, irrational forces in both himself and his world on the other. We may be tempted to identify the first set of attitudes with Creon, with his secular rationalism, confidence, and lack of reverence.[6] But the tragic position of Antigone also lies in her own miscalculation. Both figures become more human as the play progresses. Antigone, confronting the reality of her terrible punishment, laments the losses of her life. She gives as her final reason for defying Creon not the laws of Zeus of the Lower World (450ff.:494ff.) but her special tie of blood to her brother (901–15:958–73).[7] Creon, totally crushed and bereft, enters the 'Harbor of Hades' (1284:1361) and the pollutions that he was so sure about defining in rational, manageable ways (1040–44:1099–1104).

OEDIPUS TYRANNUS (OEDIPUS THE KING)

Oedipus Tyrannus is Sophocles' most famous play and the most celebrated play of Greek drama. In the *Poetics* Aristotle cites it as the best model for a tragic plot, thanks to the skill with which the recognition (*anagnôrisis*) and reversal (*peripeteia*) are interwoven. In his *Interpretation of Dreams* (1901), Sigmund Freud draws upon it for his conception of the 'oedipus complex', the son's unconscious desire to kill his father and marry his mother. The oracle that predicts Oedipus' crimes, Freud suggests, corresponds to a 'voice within us ready to recognize the compelling force of destiny'. Whatever the limits of his interpretation, Freud showed profound insight in comparing the movement of the play to the process of psychoanalysis. He thereby recognized the play's power to dramatize the process by which we uncover hidden truths about ourselves.

Why should a man or woman of noble character and good intentions have to bear a life of suffering? All of Sophocles' plays ask this question; but of the surviving seven the *Tyrannus* most profoundly probes the problem of innocent suffering and best uses the triangular relation between character, circumstances, and divine agency to answer it. In its probable order of composition, *OT* is the first of Sophocles' plays to carry its central protagonist through to the end. The three earlier plays are bisected by the protagonist's suicide before the end of the drama (Ajax, Antigone, Deianeira in *Trachinian Women*); hence they are sometimes (rather misleadingly) called 'diptych' plays. In the *Tyrannus* for the first time in Sophocles the protagonist reaches beyond suffering and bitterness to attain a self-knowledge and moral responsibility that will continue in this life.

The *Tyrannus* is commonly seen as a tragedy of inexorable Fate. The notion is foreign to the Greeks of Sophocles' time; but that effect is due in part to the extraordinary tightness of the plot. As a good king and energetic ruler, Oedipus responds to his subjects' suffering from the disastrous plague in Thebes. He sends to Apollo's oracle at Delphi and receives the oracular command, 'Drive out a pollution from the land' (97-8), which he interprets as referring to the polluting effect of the old king Laius' murder and the continuing presence of the killer in the city. As Oedipus follows the 'difficult trace of the old crime' (109), he is led back to two older oracles, the one given to Laius and Jocasta at the birth of their son and the one given to himself at Delphi, that he must kill his father and marry his mother. Jocasta's chance mention of the triple road where Laius was killed abruptly turns Oedipus' search for the murderer into a search for his own origins. From the first flutter of disturbance at Jocasta's story (727) to the moment of 'terrible hearing' when the Old Herdsman gives him the last, conclusive piece of evidence (1169-70), we watch the powerful king change from confidence and control to anxiety and utter terror.

The climax of his relentless progression toward the discovery breaks upon us in a superbly crafted movement of delay and suspense. There is no more gripping contrast in Greek drama than that between Jocasta's barely suppressed horror as she recognizes the truth and Oedipus' boastful ignorance as he lets her go to 'find her joy in her rich family' while he, as he thinks, will prove 'a child of Fortune, beneficent Fortune' (1068-85). His mood of confidence, hope, and self-deception is echoed in the chorus' ode of misplaced exultation as it speculates that he is the child of a god and a mountain nymph (1086-1109). His step-by-step interrogation of the Herdsman finally brings the terrible crash of his agony; and he rushes from the stage not in silence, like Jocasta, but with a terrible cry of comprehension (1182-5):

O, O, O, they will all come,
all come out clearly! Light of the sun, let me
look upon you no more after today!

An audience hearing these lines (and especially knowing Sophocles' previous work) would easily suppose that Oedipus, like Ajax, Deianeira, and Jocasta, is going to kill himself. Thus Oedipus' return to the stage after the Messenger's detailed account of the events in the palace must have been a stunning *coup de théâtre*, reinforced by the mask of the bloody eyes that he now wears (1297ff.).

The play does not end with Oedipus' discovery and self-blinding but goes on for some three hundred lines, in which he finds the courage to stay alive and endure the burden of his sufferings: 'No man but I can bear my evil doom' (1415). He can even see beyond the bitterness of his own life to embrace his daughters in compassion for the wretched future that awaits them.

The absorbing rhythm of discovery gains deeper resonances of meaning from the repeated references to an ever-present but mysterious background: the past of Laius, Jocasta, and Oedipus himself, the mysterious Sphinx and the plague, and the oracles. This mixture of strong surface clarity and suggestive background detail contributes to keeping open the questions about the world-order, the role of the gods in human life, and the extent to which one's whole life may be determined by a pattern established at birth or may be the result of luck and chance.

The *Tyrannus* has been read in many different ways: as a criticism of the rationalistic humanism of the Periclean Age and the Sophistic Enlightenment; as a critical or compassion-ate portrait of Pericles himself, whose ambitious hopes for Athens are shattered by the plague that killed him and weakened the city; as a tragic portrait of Athens, proud, powerful, intellectual, but like all human creations subject to the sudden vicissitudes of the uncontrollable and irrational. It is also a play about the limits and deceptiveness of language and communication. In Sophocles' celebrated 'tragic irony' words have meanings far beyond what the characters who utter them can see, as when Oedipus unknowingly curses himself and then promises to fight in defense of the murdered Laius 'as for my father' (246ff., 264). Oedipus' very name is the source of numerous puns and double-entendres, for it can be understood as 'swollen foot' (*oidein, pous*), 'know foot' (*oida pous*), 'know where' (*oida pou*: cf. 924-6), or even 'the giver knows' (*oid' ho dous*, 1038).

Closely related to the play's preoccupation with the ambiguities of language is its concern with the paradoxes of reason and knowledge. The man who can apply his intelligence so forcefully to the problems outside himself does not know the fundamental secret of who he is. His identity turns out to be a riddle more perplexing than that of the Sphinx. Oedipus could guess that the three terms of the riddle (going on four, two, and three feet) all refer to one thing, man. But he cannot see that beneath the single word 'Oedipus' are also concealed multiple beings who coexist simultaneously like the 'man' of the riddle. Oedipus' keen intelligence operates with the logic of mutually exclusive opposites: 'One man cannot be the same as many' (845). On this reckoning he bases his hope that he is not Laius' killer because the sole witness reported a multitude of attackers (122-3). But in fact Oedipus is a combination of opposites. He is simultaneously 'one' and 'many', king and pollution of his city, great ruler and worst criminal, son and husband, the outsider and the all-too-intimate member of Thebes' royal house.

For Sophocles and his contemporaries, he is the example par excellence of tragic humanity, man defined as *ephêmeros*, not 'ephemeral' in our sense but subject to the precariousness of chance, one whose fortunes may be reversed by the events of a single day (*hêmera*). The word 'day', like the related 'time', resounds ominously throughout the play. In the course of a single day, as Teiresias prophesies (351ff., 438), Oedipus goes from the height of power, wealth, and good fortune to the nadir of misery and suffering. By the end of the play, Oedipus exchanges his external, physical vision for a blindness that brings with it, at last, freedom from illusion and a clear sight of the truth about himself. The hardest of the hero's trials is, ultimately, not to defeat the Sphinx but to break through the illusions that surround his life and find the reality beneath. Sophocles has transposed the old heroic combat between man and monster to a deeper inner, tragic struggle between illusion and truth.

In the course of the play Oedipus reaches backward from maturity to childhood and forward to old age (cf. 454–6), and thus answers again in his own life and in the present the Sphinx's riddle, which confused the stages of life. The paradoxes surrounding Oedipus make him the ideal figure for exploring the human condition in its tragic dimension. Man in his intellectual power dominates the world but also by his very being is a transgressive figure. He violates the order of nature in his parricidal kingship and his incestuous marriage. He is both founder and destroyer of order, a source of strength and power, but also a source of weakness and confusion, the paradigm of cleverness and insight, but also the victim of inner blindness and lack of self-knowledge.

For the contemporary reader, Oedipus' situation touches our deepest anxieties, the possibility that life may be utterly meaningless or absurd. It is not impossible that Sophocles envisaged such a meaning too. But his concern seems to be not so much with meaninglessness as with the mysterious, ultimately unknowable shape or pattern of a life, a pattern hidden from us, yet possibly part of a larger divine scheme or plan. Everything that Oedipus does has a natural human explanation; yet everything also seems part of Apollo's design, whatever this may be.

OEDIPUS AT COLONUS

In the last years of his life Sophocles returns to the figure of Oedipus, but in a very different mood. The Oedipus of the *Coloneus* is still capable of terrible wrath and in two scenes utters the curses on his sons that will have the murderous effect that we know from *Antigone* and Aeschylus' *Seven against Thebes*. But this Oedipus enters as an aged, helpless wanderer, painfully dependent on his guide and daughter, Antigone. The side of Oedipus that could pity his daughters and weep over them in the earlier play (*OT*, 1486ff.) is more developed here; but there are also terrible depths of bitterness and anger, made sharper by the years of exile.

The repeated references to the struggle for the daily sustenance of a beggar's life reveal how changed are the circumstances of this once proud and powerful king. Yet this Oedipus has a power of another kind. He now looks to the end of his life and to its meaning in the perspective of the gods' will. He unwittingly enters the sacred grove of the dread goddesses, the Eumenides, the 'kindly ones', a gentler form of the Furies, whom he reverently addresses as 'sweet daughters of ancient Darkness' (106:118), and realizes that this will be his final resting place. The play begins and ends in or near this grove; and there is a mysterious affinity between the fear inspired by these divinities and that aroused by Oedipus himself. Both are called 'terrible', *deinos*, and both are the source of curses and blessings.

In entering the sacred place of goddesses associated with the earth and the vengeance for crimes against the family, Oedipus symbolically re-enacts his earlier transgression; but it is a sign of the reconciliation with the gods that now attends him that these dread divinities are a source of comfort. Oedipus' concern to propitiate the goddesses is not only in strong contrast with the doubting and hesitation about the gods in the *Tyrannus*; it is also an external manifestation of an inner purification. He is not morally guilty, he insists, because he committed the parricide and incest ignorantly and unintentionally (266–74, 521–48, 960–1002:278–88, 584–625, 1104–53).

Ritual purification frames the action of the play. The propitiatory rituals that Oedipus would perform to the Eumenides are interrupted by Creon's violence in the middle of the play and are successfully resumed at the end. The purification of Oedipus takes the two-fold form of separating him from his polluted, Theban past and from the Thebans who would pull him back into it – for their advantage, not his. The kindness and piety of Theseus will incorporate him into his new homeland of Athens, and the Eumenides' grove at Athens' frontier is the point of entrance and mysterious transition. Here he will be a savior to Athens and a protector against its enemies. The mysterious power that will radiate from his miserable, aged body (109–10:121–2) will be denied to the Thebans and instead will benefit Athens.

Sophocles here draws on the complex of Greek religious notions of hero-cult, as he had in the *Ajax*, some fifty years earlier. He himself, we recall, received such a cult after his death. 'Heroes', in this technical sense, are mortal high achievers whose life-story is generally embedded in old myths or legends. Their extraordinary force and passion lead them to actions beyond the limits of normal humanity and often bring them into conflict with human and divine laws. Hence they perform great outrages as well as great benefactions. They generally come to a violent and mysterious end in which the paradoxes of transgression and greatness are enacted in a supernatural event like sudden disappearance or some other intervention by the gods.

The *Coloneus* is in effect an aetiological myth to explain the local cult of Oedipus in Sophocles' home town of Colonus, but the hero-cult is also appropriate to the paradoxes of Oedipus' life and character. The cult-hero's ambiguous place between criminality and nobility projects into ritual and religious terms Oedipus' ambiguity between guilt and innocence, bitter resentment and prophetic grandeur. The gods, so remote and even malevolent-seeming in the *Tyrannus*, now offer him rest from his terrible curse and the burden of his life. Whereas the polluted Oedipus of the earlier play had no place under the sun (*OT*, 1425–31), the powers of both earth and sky now acquiesce in his burial (*OC*, 1653–62:1876–86).

Alongside the religious dimension of the play, however, political themes continue to surround this once great ruler. Oedipus remains linked with the political life of a city. His burial is possible because he has found his way to a just city and a pious king. The play operates with the pervasive contrast of the accursed city of Thebes, marked by civil and family strife, and Athens, where the old Furies dwell as Eumenides in their beautiful grove and do not go forth to wreak their horrible vengeance on men and women as do the Furies in the house of Oedipus at Thebes (see *Antigone*, 597–603:652–6).

In contrasting a city of peace and piety with a city haunted by curses and blood pollution and in transforming the Furies' wrath into a kindly force that can coexist with civic life, the *Coloneus* has affinities with Aeschylus' *Oresteia*. As at the end of the *Oresteia*, men are reconciled with the harsh divinities of family vengeance; and a city engulfed by violence (Aeschylus' Argos, Sophocles' Thebes) gives way to a city of peace and justice (Athens). But in Aeschylus what makes the transition possible is the mechanism of justice at the Areopagus and the persuasive intervention of Athena (whatever its problems for the justice of the Furies' claims), whereas the *Coloneus* emphasizes the hero himself, his special relation with the gods, and the mysterious divine voice that finally calls him by name to his place beyond the limits of human laws. We are told of Theseus' awed response – he is the sole witness of the mystery (1647–57:1870–80) – and we know that it is for Oedipus more than for Thebes or Athens that the gods have made this miraculous incursion into the fabric of ordinary reality. We are in a different world from the bleak prospect of suffering and Oedipus' bitter acceptance of it in the *Tyrannus*:

Yet I know this much:
no sickness and no other thing will kill me.
I would not have been saved from death if not
for some strange evil fate. Well, let my fate
go where it will. (*OT*, 1455–8).

Nothing in the earlier play would have led one to expect this mysterious dispensation of the gods in the later.

Sophocles might have ended the play with the reverent gestures of Theseus and the mysterious signs of the gods' reconciliation with Oedipus. Instead, he returns to the suffering that remains within the family and the city of Oedipus' birth. Theseus can protect Oedipus and his daughters from Creon, but he cannot protect the two daughters from the bitterness and violence that still reach out to them from Thebes. Rejecting Theseus' offer of hospitality in Athens, Ismene and Antigone decide to return to 'primordial Thebes' (1769–70:2013–15) and so fulfill the curse on the house of Laius. The play ends, then, where Sophocles' first Theban play began, with the sisters' involvement in the divisions within the city and family of Thebes.

Always intensely involved with his city, Sophocles writes his last play when its energies are exhausted and its territory repeatedly ravaged by the invading Spartan forces. The beautiful poetry that describes the grove of the Eumenides at Colonus (668–719:765–813) restores to this weakened Athens an integrity and inviolability that symbolically counteract the contemporary vulnerability of her physical boundaries. If the Oedipus of the *Tyrannus* embodies to some extent the proud, powerful Athens at the height of the Periclean Age, the Oedipus of the *Coloneus* reflects the Athens of the last years of the Peloponnesian War, outwardly depleted and enfeebled, encompassed on all sides by hatred and enmity, yet possessed of a mysterious inner strength and a spiritual power that receive ultimate recognition from the gentled, if still terrible, goddesses of the grove.[8]

The Thebes of the *Antigone* and *Tyrannus* receives dire warnings in the form of plague and pollutions because men in their pride and confidence forget the limits of human power. Athens in the *Coloneus* is at peace with the gods. The Athens of this play, like that of the *Oresteia*, finds a place for those female powers of earth and creation that the grove at Colonus shelters and hallows.

The choral ode that describes the sanctity of the Eumenides' grove at Colonus in the middle of the play (668–719:765–813) spans the two forces that Sophoclean tragedy explores and brings into the city. It is a sunless, windless place, hedged about by warnings against trespassing; but it is also full of the life of nature: burgeoning vegetation, flowers, birds, flowing water, song and music, even Aphrodite. It is a place of crossing between life and death, upper and lower worlds, earth and sea; and it is also uniquely Athenian, protected by Athens' goddess and partaking of the uninterrupted continuity of habitation in the ancient land, in which the autochthonous Athenians took special pride (694–706:789–802).

SOPHOCLES AND THE GODS

Sophocles was considered pious by his contemporaries, but it is not easy to define just what that piety was. Like his fellow-tragedians, Aeschylus and Euripides, he is deeply interested in the performance of ritual and the details of ritual. In *Antigone*, for instance, the Guard makes a point of the efficacy of the sprinkled dust on Polyneices' body (256:282–3); and Teiresias offers a detailed account of the omens and ritual disorder on the altars and in the skies (998–1022:1052–72). The *Oedipus at Colonus* painstakingly describes how Oedipus must propitiate the Eumenides (468–92:523–49). But such rites are only a framework for the questions of justice and the meaning of life that Sophocles explores through the relation between men and gods.

The Greek gods, we must recall, are not the beneficent creators of the world, but rather beings who express its timelessness and order, and the interconnection between its parts. Sophocles often emphasizes the gap between these remote gods who maintain the world order and mortals involved in time and change (e.g. *Antigone*, 604–14:657–66, and *OT*, 863–72). Both of these passages identify a general notion of divinity ('god', *theos*) with Zeus and Olympus. They contrast this ageless divine power and law with the changefulness of human life and man's tendency to error and wrongdoing. Such gods reveal themselves by their mysterious and unpredictable presence in the human world. Indeed, it is sometimes the mere possibility of such divine presence that interests Sophocles, the indications, generally noticed only too late, that human life is surrounded by forces beyond what most men can see. Those who do see are set apart in a vision of their own, like the blind prophet Teiresias ('in whom alone of mankind truth is native', *OT* 299), and the aged sufferer Oedipus at the end of his life, who in his blindness has been granted the vision of a prophet (*OC* 1540ff.:1758ff.).

Divine presence is always mysterious. The *Antigone*, for instance, never tells us for certain who or what buried Polyneices for the first time. The Guard is baffled by the lack of any physical evidence and calls the event a 'wonder' or 'marvel' (*thauma*, 249–54:273–85):

... there was there no mark
of axe's stroke nor casting up of earth

of any mattock; the ground was hard and dry,
unbroken; there were no signs of wagon wheels.
The doer of the deed had left no trace.
But when the first sentry of the day pointed it out,
there was for all of us a disagreeable
wonder. For the body had disappeared;
not in a grave, of course; but there lay upon him
a little dust as of a hand avoiding
the curse of violating the dead body's sanctity.
There were no signs of any beast nor dog
that came there; he had clearly not been torn.

The fact that the deed took place while it was still night, when
Antigone was still planning it with Ismene in the prologue
(16:17), has been taken to indicate that she could not have
performed this first burial. The chorus in fact raises the
possibility that the burial is an act of the gods (278:308), a
view that infuriates Creon, who is so sure about what the gods
want. Even the second burial of Polyneices, when Antigone is
caught in the act, is accompanied by strange events on the face
of nature. There is a mysterious co-operation between her
desperate attempt to sprinkle dust on the body and a swirling
of dust in the heavens that 'fills the plain' and is 'a disease from
the gods' and 'a grief in the heavens'. It is as if Antigone's act is
magnified into cosmic proportions, and it is out of this dust-
filled cloud that Antigone suddenly appears (417–23:458–65).
In neither of these passages is a specific divinity named. It is
perhaps enough for Sophocles to suggest that human lives are
always a part of some larger pattern, a pattern whose meaning
is the meaning of the gods.

In the case of the *Tyrannus* too, although Apollo and his
oracles are ever-present, we are never actually told that
Apollo has caused these events. Oedipus' first utterance, when
he returns to the stage after the terrible events inside, is a cry,
amid the paroxysms of his pain, to a 'divinity' that 'leapt out
at him' (1311), as chance or misfortune leapt upon the head of
Laius (263; cf. 469). A few lines later, Oedipus attributes his
sufferings to Apollo, but even here he distinguishes between
the sufferings that came from the god, that is, from sources
beyond his control, and his own deliberately chosen act of

tearing out his eyes (1329–35). And behind Apollo stands Zeus, who is mentioned in almost every ode of the play. The one exception is the ode that proves to be disastrously mistaken in its optimistic view of playful, anthropomorphic gods (1086–1109). Zeus emerges as the remote, inscrutable god of the world order, 'ruler of all things' (904), as he is in the third ode of *Antigone* (604ff.:640ff.). Though Apollo and his oracle dominate Oedipus' thoughts, he cries out to Zeus when Jocasta tells her story and gives him the first glimpse of the horror lurking behind his power and prosperity: 'What have you designed, O Zeus, to do with me?' (738). The answer comes at the very end of his life when Zeus' signs from the heavens set the hero in seeing blindness upon his last journey and the fulfillment of his destiny (*OC*, 1456–71, 1485: 1672–87, 1699).

As the examples of Antigone and Oedipus show, it is primarily through his characters that Sophocles speculates on the nature of the gods. He explores the special relation that comes into being between the gods and the men and women whose extraordinary force, energy, commitment, or excess call divinity into their lives. Their suffering raises questions of ultimate meaning precisely because it stands close to the eternal powers that govern the workings of the world. Some heroes, like Oedipus, are marked out at birth for a suffering that does not seem to have a rational human explanation, although they themselves co-operate in the fulfillment of this suffering through their own natures. Others, like Ajax, Antigone, or Electra, refuse to compromise with conditions that they perceive as unjust or dishonorable. Rejecting a life of safe quiescence or comfortable passivity, they are doomed to suffer because of an irresolvable conflict between their own natures and the world as they see it. Sophocles seems to have regarded life itself as tragic because the energies, passions, errors, and fluctuations inherent in human nature clash with the way the world is constituted, with the realities enforced by the gods. The heroes are the initiators of this conflict and of the suffering that it causes, but the conflagration always spreads to other, innocent lives – Haemon, Eurydice, Jocasta.

Sophocles' technique is to allow events to develop fully and naturally from human motives and human character rather than from divine intervention. Only once in the seven surviving plays does a divinity appear on-stage, namely Athena in the *Ajax*; and her unpitying vindictiveness horrifies even her human protégé, Ajax's greatest enemy, the cautious Odysseus (*Ajax*, 118–33).[9] Even in *Antigone*, where piety toward the gods of the lower world is so clearly vindicated, the gods do not directly intervene. They operate obscurely, at a distance, but they do seem to ensure a kind of order in the world, even though that order is not always fully intelligible in human terms or gentle to the innocent. In a general way the gods are identified with the forces in nature that restore to equilibrium the balances disturbed by man. The plague that kills so many in Thebes makes manifest in all of nature the fearful pollution inside the house and body of Oedipus. But the elimination of the pollution, as in the *Antigone*, does not necessarily discriminate degrees of guilt or innocence. Oedipus and Antigone both suffer far more than human justice would seem to require.

Whatever Sophocles' personal religion, the plays by no means show a simple reverence or piety. The supernatural elements in his plays generally pose questions rather than give answers. He does not commit himself either to attacking or defending the gods. They simply *are*, and their presence in the background of every play suggests the existence of mysterious forces that give a human life the form that it has in the final order of things, which the gods embody. Only the great heroes come to perceive the shape that their lives must fulfill; and only they have the strength, like Antigone and Oedipus, to grasp that destiny and see it through with courage and clarity to the end.

Charles Segal

NOTES

———

1 Quoted in Hypothesis II of *Oedipus at Colonus*, from Phrynichus, *The Muses*, fragment 32, in R. Kassel and C. Austin, eds., *Poetae Comici Graeci*, vol. 7, De Gruyter, Berlin and New York, 1989.

2 Text and translation in David A. Campbell, ed., *Greek Lyric*, vol. 3, Loeb Classical Library, Harvard University Press, Cambridge, MA, 1991, 136–43. For discussion see Segal, 'Archaic Choral Lyric', in *Cambridge History of Classical Literature*, 1: 197–200.

3 Except for a few short phrases I cite Grene's translation from this volume, but in the case of *Antigone* and *Oedipus at Colonus* I also give the standard line numbers of the Greek text in addition to the line numbers of Grene's translation (this is not necessary in the case of his translation of *Oedipus Tyrannus*, which closely follows the Greek line numbers). The medieval manuscripts attribute to Antigone line 572 (=630 Grene, 'Dear Haemon, how your father dishonors you'). Grene's translation follows the manuscripts; but the attribution of speakers in the manuscripts does not go back to the author and is sometimes mistaken. With many editors I believe that the line must be spoken by Ismene. For the arguments pro and con see the commentaries of Jebb and Kamerbeek *ad loc.*

4 It is still a matter of controversy whether this ending of the *Seven* was part of Aeschylus' original play or, as many scholars think, was added later, under the influence of Sophocles' *Antigone*.

5 See Richard Seaford, 'The Tragic Wedding', *Journal of Hellenic Studies* 107 (1987), 106–30, especially 106–8; see also Segal, *Tragedy and Civilization*, 177ff.

6 Segal, *Interpreting Greek Tragedy*, 141ff.

7 The genuineness of these lines is sometimes questioned, but there are no compelling reasons against them, and recent commentators increasingly accept them.

8 See Knox, *Heroic Temper*, 155–6; Segal, *Tragedy and Civilization*, 407–8.

9 The appearance of the divinized Heracles at the end of *Philoctetes* is more a manifestation of the protagonist's lost heroism than a representation of an independent divine power.

SELECT BIBLIOGRAPHY

EDITIONS AND COMMENTARIES:
DAWE, R.D., *Sophocles: Oedipus Tyrannus*, Cambridge: Cambridge University Press, 1982. Detailed linguistic commentary.

HOGAN, JAMES C., *A Commentary on the Plays of Sophocles*, Carbondale and Edwardsville: Southern Illinois University Press, Illinois, 1991. Helpful explanatory and interpretative notes for the general reader, based on the Grene-Lattimore translations. Covers all seven of the extant plays.

JEBB, RICHARD C., *Sophocles: The Plays and Fragments*, 7 volumes, Cambridge: Cambridge University Press, 1892–1907. Useful introductions, Greek text, facing prose translations, and commentary. Still valuable.

KAMERBEEK, J.C., *The Plays of Sophocles*, 7 volumes, Leiden: Brill, 1953–84. Primarily linguistic commentary, with useful introductions.

LLOYD-JONES, HUGH, and WILSON, N.G., *Sophoclis Fabulae*, Oxford Classical Texts, Oxford: Clarendon Press, 1990. The standard Greek text of Sophocles.

TRANSLATIONS
FAGLES, ROBERT, *Sophocles, The Three Theban Plays*, Harmondsworth and New York: Penguin Classics, 1984. Contains introductory essays by Bernard Knox.

GRENE, DAVID, and LATTIMORE, RICHMOND: eds., *The Complete Greek Tragedies*, Chicago: University of Chicago Press, 1954–9, 2nd edn 1990–92, 4 volumes: vol. 1, Aeschylus; vol. 2, Sophocles; vols. 3–4, Euripides.

THE GREEK THEATER: HISTORICAL AND INTELLECTUAL BACKGROUND
BALDRY, H.C., *The Greek Tragic Theater*, London: Chatto and Windus, 1971. A concise introduction to the main features of the ancient performances for the general reader.

BIEBER, MARGARETE, *The History of the Greek and Roman Theater*, 2nd edn, Princeton: Princeton University Press, 1961. Detailed account of physical remains of the Greek theaters and of the archaeological evidence for the staging, masks, costumes, etc., with helpful illustrations.

BURN, A.R., *Pericles and Athens*, New York: Collier, 1962. Brief account of the political and cultural history of Athens in the Periclean age, for the general reader.

CARTLEDGE, PAUL, *The Greeks*, Oxford: Oxford University Press, 1993. Contemporary, non-idealizing decription of Greek culture taking an anthropological approach and emphasizing the Greeks' conceptual construction of their world through contrast and parallelism.

EASTERLING, P.E., and KNOX, B.M.W., eds. *Cambridge History of Classical Literature*, vol. 1., Cambridge: Cambridge University Press, 1985. (Also published in separate fascicles: Part 2 is *Greek Drama*.) General history of Greek literature with chapters on the Greek theater and the individual tragedians and useful chronologies and bibliographies.

GUTHRIE, W.K.C., *A History of Greek Philosophy*, vols. 2 and 3, Cambridge: Cambridge University Press, 1965, 1969. Detailed account of the Sophists, Socrates, and other thinkers contemporary with Sophocles.

RODENWALDT, GERHART, and HEGE, WALTER, *The Acropolis*, 2nd edn., Oxford: Blackwell, 1957. Well-illustrated account of the Parthenon and other buildings on the Acropolis in the Periclean Age.

HAMMOND, N.G.L., *A History of Greece to 322 BC*, 2nd edn., Oxford: Clarendon Press, 1967. An authoritative history of Greece, including the Periclean Age.

PICKARD-CAMBRIDGE, ARTHUR W., *Dithyramb, Tragedy and Comedy*, 2nd edn., Rev. T.B.L. Webster, Oxford: Oxford University Press, 1962.
– – -. *The Dramatic Festivals of Athens*, 2nd edn., Rev. John Gould and D.M. Lewis, Oxford: Oxford University Press, 1968.
– – -. *The Theater of Dionysus at Athens*, Oxford: Oxford University Press, 1946. These three works provide the most authoritative general discussions of the origins and material background of Greek tragedy and the festivals at which the plays were performed. Sometimes rather technical.

CRITICAL STUDIES.

BOWRA, C.M., *Sophoclean Tragedy*, Oxford: Oxford University Press, 1944. A play-by-play reading of Sophocles, with a heavily moralizing approach.

BURIAN, PETER. 'Suppliant and Savior: Oedipus at Colonus', *Phoenix* 28 (1974): 408–29. Emphasizes the importance of the hero cult in *OC*.

BUXTON, R.G.A., *Sophocles, Greece & Rome*, Supplement, *New Surveys in the Classics*, No. 16. Oxford: Clarendon Press, 1984. Useful brief survey of recent writing on Sophocles.

DODDS, E.R., 'On Misunderstanding the *Oedipus Rex*', *Greece & Rome* 13 (1966): 37–49 (reprinted in O'Brien, below). Influential essay, challenging the conventional approaches to the play and emphasizing Oedipus' moral innocence and the problem of irrational suffering and the gods in Sophocles.

EDMUNDS, LOWELL, ed., *Oedipus: The Ancient Legend and its Later Analogues*, Baltimore: Johns Hopkins University Press, 1984.

– – –. and Alan Dundes, *Oedipus: A Folklore Casebook*, New York: Garland, 1983. These two books contain valuable collections of comparative material and discuss the Oedipus myth and myths of the Oedipus type in Europe and other societies.

EHRENBERG, VICTOR, *Sophocles and Pericles*, Oxford: Blackwell, 1954. Argues for a conservative Sophocles, whose Oedipus in *OT* is a warning about Pericles' secular rationalism and confidence.

GARDINER, CYNTHIA P, *The Sophoclean Chorus*, Iowa City: University of Iowa Press, 1987. Close study of the chorus as a character with a distinctive personality in Sophocles. Includes a chapter on the Theban plays.

GOLDHILL, SIMON, *Reading Greek Tragedy*, Cambridge: Cambridge University Press, 1986. Stimulating essays on Greek drama, using contemporary critical theories. Includes discussions of *Antigone* and *OT*.

JONES, JOHN, *On Aristotle and Greek Tragedy*, London: Chatto and Windus, 1962. Argues for the primacy of action and event over the modern conception of character in Greek tragedy.

KIRKWOOD, G.M, *A Study of Sophoclean Drama*, Ithaca: Cornell University Press, 1958. Useful topic-by-topic study of Sophoclean dramaturgy through a cross-section of the plays.

KNOX, B.M.W, *Oedipus at Thebes*, New Haven: Yale University Press, 1957. A pioneering study of Sophocles' language, based on the 'new criticism'. Argues that the tragedy of Oedipus in the *OT* reflects the dangers of Athens at the height of its power and confidence under Pericles.

– – –. *The Heroic Temper: Studies in Sophoclean Tragedy*, Berkeley and Los Angeles: University of California Press, 1964. A close study of the tragic personality of the Sophoclean hero, emphasizing the mixture of nobility and grandeur with violence and an obsessive concern with honor. Contains two detailed chapters on *Antigone*.

– – –.*Word and Action: Essays on the Ancient Theatre*, Baltimore and London: Johns Hopkins University Press, 1979. Includes essays on the dating, historical circumstances, and staging of *OT*.

LATTIMORE, RICHMOND, *The Poetry of Greek Tragedy*, Baltimore: Johns Hopkins University Press, 1958. Contains a useful discussion of the foundling theme in *OT*.

O'BRIEN, MICHAEL J, *Twentieth Century Interpretations of Oedipus Rex*,

THE THEBAN PLAYS

Englewood Cliffs, N.J.: Prentice-Hall, 1968. An anthology of essays and critical statements about *OT*, including Dodds' essay (above).

POOLE, ADRIAN, *Tragedy, Shakespeare and the Greek Example*, Oxford: Blackwell, 1986. Literary commentary on *OT* and *Antigone*, using comparison with Shakespeare to define the distinctively Greek quality of the tragic experience.

REINHARDT, KARL, *Sophocles*, trans. H. and D. Harvey, Oxford: Blackwell, 1979. A celebrated study of Sophocles, containing insightful scene-by-scene analyses of the seven plays in a philosophical spirit. Emphasizes the clash between illusion and reality, the evolution of Sophocles' dramaturgy, and his world-view in comparison to Aeschylus and Euripides.

RUDNYTSKY, PETER L, *Freud and Oedipus*, New York: Columbia University Press, 1987. Detailed study of Freud's approach to *OT* and its intellectual background in the nineteenth century. Includes a contemporary psychoanalytic reading of the Theban plays.

SCODEL, RUTH, *Sophocles*, Boston: Twayne World Authors Series, 1984. A brief, non-specialist introduction to Sophocles, with chapters on each of the seven plays.

SEGAL, CHARLES, *Tragedy and Civilization: An Interpretation of Sophocles*, Cambridge, MA: Harvard University Press, 1981. A detailed play-by-play study of all of Sophocles, focusing on the triangular relations between human nature, society, and the world-order. Drawing on structural anthropology, the book is especially concerned with Sophocles' use of ritual and mythical patterns in presenting the contradictions inherent in human life.

— — -. 'Sophocles', *Ancient Writers: Greece and Rome*, ed. T.J. Luce, New York: Scribners, 1982, vol. 1: 179–207. A brief introduction to all of Sophocles.

— — -. *Interpreting Greek Tragedy*, Ithaca: Cornell University Press, 1986. Essays on Greek drama in the perspective of contemporary criticism. Includes discussions of *OT*, *Antigone*, and visual symbolism in Sophocles.

— — -. *Oedipus Tyrannus: Tragic Heroism and the Limits of Knowledge*, New York: Twayne – Macmillan, 1993. Contains a close, scene-by-scene reading of the play in the light of the problem of knowledge and the hero. Includes chapters on the historical, intellectual, literary, and mythical background and on the play's later interpretations and its influence on modern literature and art.

STEINER, GEORGE, *Antigones*, Oxford: Oxford University Press, 1984. Studies the continuities and transformations of *Antigone* in modern literature and thought, especially in the nineteenth and twentieth centuries, with some interesting reflections on Sophocles' play.

SELECT BIBLIOGRAPHY

TAPLIN, OLIVER, *Greek Tragedy in Action*, Berkeley and Los Angeles: University of California Press, 1978. Readable account of Greek drama, especially of its visual and theatrical effects.

VERNANT, JEAN-PIERRE, and VIDAL-NAQUET, P, *Myth and Tragedy in Ancient Greece*, trans. J. Lloyd, New York: Zone Books, 1990. Stimulating essays exploring the mythical structures implicit in Greek tragedy. Argues for tragedy's role in the *polis* as a means of critical reflection on contemporary social and political institutions. Includes several detailed studies of *OT* and *OC*.

WHITMAN, C.H, *Sophocles: A Study of Heroic Humanism*, Cambridge, MA: Harvard University Press, 1951. Elegantly written study, challenging the 'tragic flaw' approach and emphasizing the individual hero's moral and spiritual greatness in an irrational world. Needs to be balanced by the darker views of the hero in Knox and Winnington-Ingram.

WINNINGTON-INGRAM, R.P, *Sophocles: An Interpretation*, Cambridge: Cambridge University Press, 1980. A fine study of critical problems in Sophocles, with detailed chapters on the Theban plays. Emphasizes the dangerous and violent side of the hero, the continuities between Aeschylus and Sophocles, and Sophocles' indebtedness to the archaic religion and world-view.

CHRONOLOGY

DATE	AUTHOR'S LIFE	LITERARY CONTEXT
525 BC		Birth of Aeschylus.
515 BC		Birth of Parmenides in Elea, southern Italy – author of *On Nature* of which only fragments survive.
500 BC		Heraclitus thought to have flourished at this time.
499– 494 BC		
498 BC		Pindar: *Pythian X*.
c. 497 BC	Birth of Sophocles in Colonus, the son of Sophilus, a wealthy manufacturer of armour. 123 plays are ascribed to Sophocles of which only seven survive.	
490 BC		Simonides' epitaph on the Athenian dead at Marathon, preferred to that of Aeschylus who had fought there.
485 BC		Birth of Euripides.
484 BC		Birth of Herodotus, Greek historian.
483 BC		
480 BC	Sophocles chosen to lead the chorus which sang the paean in honour of the Greek victory at Salamis.	
479 BC		
478 BC		
476 BC		Death of Hecataeus of Miletus, historian and geographer. Odes of Pindar and Bacchylides commemorate the victory of Hieron, tyrant of Syracuse, in the horse-race at the Olympian Games.
472 BC		Aeschylus: *Persae*. It is thought that Pythagoras died about this time, aged ninety-nine.

Birth of Pheidias, Greek sculptor.

Ionian revolt from the Persians.

Birth of Pericles, Athenian statesman. Persian invasion of Sparta. Battle of Marathon.

Death of Darius, ruler of Persia. He is succeeded by his son, Xerxes.

Themistocles becomes political leader in Athens.
Battles of Artemisium and Thermopylae. Athens sacked by Persian army.
Persian fleet defeated at Salamis.

The Great Wall of Themistocles is built.
The Persian army defeated at Plataea.
Xanthippus commands the victorious Athenian fleet at Mycale.
Delian League against Persia founded by Greeks under Athenian leadership –
the origin of the Athenian Empire.

DATE	AUTHOR'S LIFE	LITERARY CONTEXT
471 BC		
470 BC		
469 BC		Birth of Socrates.
468 BC	Sophocles, with *Triptolemus* and two other plays, achieves his first victory over Aeschylus in the annual competition of tragic poets held during the Great Dionysia.	
467 BC		Aeschylus' Oedipus trilogy (of which only *Seven against Thebes* survives).
464 BC		Anaxagoras (b. 500 BC), Greek philosopher, is thought to have come to Athens about this time. His pupils include Pericles, Euripides, and perhaps Socrates.
461 BC		
460 BC	*Ajax* (to 450).	Birth of Democritus, Greek philosopher. Birth of Hippocrates, Greek physician – to him is ascribed the Hippocratic oath, earliest and most impressive statement on medical ethics.
458 BC		Aeschylus: *Oresteia*.
457 BC		
456 BC		Death of Aeschylus.
455 BC		Euripides begins his dramatic career, winning third place in drama competition with *Pleiades*. Birth of Thucydides, son of Olorus, author of *History of the Peloponnesian War*. Birth of Antisthenes, Greek philosopher and pupil of Socrates.
450-390 BC		The period of Old Comedy, characterized by broad and undisguised raillery of contemporary events and living persons.

xlii

CHRONOLOGY

Themistocles ostracized and banished from Athens.

Cimon, in sole command of the Greek fleet, conquers the island of Scyros.

Pericles considered to be the leader of the democratic party in opposition to Cimon.

Athenian navy under Cimon shatters the Persian fleet at the battle of the Eurymedon river in Pamphylia.

Earthquake in Sparta.

Cimon leads an Athenian force to aid Sparta when the helots revolt. His proffered aid is dismissed with scorn by the Spartans and he is ostracized by the Athenians because of this on a pretext of corruption. Pericles comes into political prominence.

Cimon is recalled to Athens to defeat the Persians off the coast of Cyprus. Although successful, he dies before the war is over.

Five Years Truce between Athens and Sparta.

DATE	AUTHOR'S LIFE	LITERARY CONTEXT
450 BC		
449 BC		
448 BC		Zeno of Elea, favourite disciple of Parmenides, arrives in Athens about this time. Aristotle was to call Zeno 'the founder of dialectic'.
447 BC		
446 BC		Last dateable ode of Pindar.
444 BC		Birth of Aristophanes.
443 BC	Sophocles serves as state supervisor of the tribute from the Athenian empire (to 442).	
441 BC	*Antigone* first produced. Sophocles elected as one of the ten *strategoi* (military and naval commanders) in the revolt of Samos (to 440). His senior colleague was Pericles.	
440 BC		A decree is passed prohibiting comedy.
440–432 BC	*Trachinian Women* (date is controversial and estimates range from 450 to 420 BC, but 440–430 is most likely).	
438 BC		Euripides: *Alcestis*. Death of Pindar (b.518 BC) – Pindar is reputed to have produced enough work to make a collection comprising seventeen books (i.e. papyrus rolls), including hymns, paeans, dithyrambs, processional songs, maiden songs, dirges and odes. Four books of victory odes and fragments of the other poems survive.
437 BC		Repeal of the prohibition on comedy.
432 BC		

CHRONOLOGY

xlv

DATE	AUTHOR'S LIFE	LITERARY CONTEXT
431 BC		Euripides produces *Medea*.
430 BC		Euripides: *Heracleidae*. Birth of Xenophon. For some years he is a pupil of Socrates. His accounts of Socrates are among the very few remaining contemporary testimonies about him. Books include: *Memorabilia* (Memoirs of Socrates), *Apology of Socrates*, and *Symposium*.
430–428 BC		
429 BC	*Oedipus Tyrannus* (to 425)	
428 BC		Death of Anaxagoras. Euripides: *Hippolytus*. Plato born in Athens.
427 BC		Gorgias of Leontini arrives in Athens as an Ambassador. He is chiefly remembered for bringing Rhetoric to Athens.
426 BC		Euripides: *Andromache*.
425 BC		Aristophanes: *The Acharnians*. Euripides: *Hecuba*. Death of Herodotus, Greek historian.
424 BC		Aristophanes: *The Knights*.
423 BC		Aristophanes: *The Clouds*, satirizing the Sophists, especially Socrates.
422 BC		Aristophanes: *The Wasps*. Euripides: *Suppliant Women*; *Electra* (to 418).
421 BC		Aristophanes: *The Peace*.
420 BC	*Electra* (to 410).	
415 BC		
414 BC		Aristophanes: *The Birds*. Euripides: *Iphigenia in Tauris*.

xlvi

CHRONOLOGY

Outbreak of the Peloponnesian War against Sparta (to 404). The campaign is led by Pericles, leading statesman of Athens, who urges the Athenians to rely wholly upon their seapower; their neglect of this advice leads ultimately to disaster.

The Great Plague of Athens in which thousands die, include Pericles and his two sons, Xanthippus and Paralus. Cleon succeeds Pericles as the most influential politician; he is opposed by Nicias.

Revolt of Lesbos.

Eruption of Mount Etna.
Death of Polygnotus (b. 500 BC), Greek painter, chiefly remembered for the 'Sack of Troy' and 'Ulysses in the Underworld'. The Athenians capture Pylos.

Death of Cleon at the battle of Amphipolis.

Peace of Nicias between Athens and Sparta. The Erechtheum built in Athens (to 406).

Athenians attempt conquest of Syracuse and Italy.
Alcibiades is forced to leave Athens after being accused of the mutilation of the images of Hermes.
Sicilian Expedition ends in disaster. Athens loses more than 30,000 men and 200 ships at Syracuse.

DATE	AUTHOR'S LIFE	LITERARY CONTEXT
413 BC	After the failure of the Sicilian Expedition, Sophocles is made one of the *probouloi* (commissioners) to deal with the crisis.	
412 BC		Birth of Diogenes (d. 323 BC), Greek philosopher.
411 BC		Aristophanes: *Lysistrata*. Xenophon begins *Hellenica*, a history of Greece that will take him some forty-nine years to complete.
410 BC		Euripides: *Ion*.
409 BC	*Philoctetes*.	
408 BC		Euripides: *Orestes*.
407 BC		Plato meets Socrates.
406 BC	*Oedipus at Colonus* written. Death of Sophocles. He receives posthumous cult as Dexion, 'the Receiver', for having received the sacred snake of the healing god Asclepius. He left two sons – Iophon the tragedian, by Nicostratë and Agathon, by Theoris of Cicyon.	Death of Euripides.
405 BC		Euripides: *Bacchae*; *Iphigenia in Aulis*. Aristophanes: *The Frogs*. Includes an hilarious fictional contest between Euripides and Aeschylus to decide who is the greatest tragedian. Aeschylus wins, Sophocles having relinquished his claim in favour of the latter.
404 BC		
402 BC	Sophocles' grandson (another Sophocles, also a tragedian) presents *Oedipus at Colonus*.	Hellanicus: *History of Attica*.

CHRONOLOGY

War resumes in mainland Greece; Spartan treaties with Persia.

Dictatorship of the Four Hundred, a revolutionary oligarchic council that seized power from the Council of Five Hundred and ruled Athens for three months, until control was seized by the so-called Government of the Five Thousand. Democracy was swiftly restored, and with it the old Council of Five Hundred. The orator Antiphon put to death for his part in the coup.

Battle of Cyzicus. Sparta makes proposals of peace which are rejected by Athens.

Chariot racing with horses introduced into the Olympic Games.
Birth of Dion of Syracuse, brother-in-law of Dionysius I.
Alcibiades is recalled to Athens.
Socrates elected to the Council of Five Hundred but he opposes them for acting contrary to the law.

Sparta attacks Athens.
Athenian fleet destroyed at Aegospotami. There follows a five month siege of the City.

Athens capitulates to Sparta after nearly thirty years of war. The Tyranny of the Thirty in Athens.

TRANSLATOR'S NOTE

———

Though the numbered lines of my *Oedipus the King* appear to match fairly thoroughly those of the Greek text, I have not been so successful with the combination of the Greek and the English in *Oedipus at Colonus* and *Antigone*. Often I have needed more space than the limitation of a line would allow. I decided that my numbering should correspond with the lines of the English translation rather than with those of the Greek, since if anyone wanted to cite a passage it would be unlikely that he or she would refer to the Greek. I hope this will not lead to too much confusion.

OEDIPUS THE KING

CHARACTERS

OEDIPUS: *King of Thebes*
JOCASTA: *His Wife*
CREON: *His Brother-in-Law*
TEIRESIAS: *an Old Blind Prophet*
A PRIEST
FIRST MESSENGER
SECOND MESSENGER
A HERDSMAN
A CHORUS OF OLD MEN OF THEBES

OEDIPUS THE KING

*In front of the palace of Oedipus at Thebes. To the right
of the stage near the altar stands the priest with a crowd
of children. Oedipus emerges from the central door.*

OEDIPUS: Children, young sons and daughters of old
    Cadmus,
why do you sit here with your suppliant crowns?
The town is heavy with a mingled burden
of sounds and smells, of groans and hymns and incense;   5
I did not think it fit that I should hear
of this from messengers but came myself,—
I Oedipus whom all men call the Great.
(*He turns to the Priest.*)
You're old and they are young; come, speak for them.
What do you fear or want, that you sit here   10
suppliant? Indeed I'm willing to give all
that you may need; I would be very hard
should I not pity suppliants like these.

PRIEST: O ruler of my country, Oedipus,
you see our company around the altar;   15
you see our ages; some of us, like these,
who cannot yet fly far, and some of us
heavy with age; these children are the chosen
among the young, and I the priest of Zeus.
Within the market place sit others crowned   20
with suppliant garlands, at the double shrine
of Pallas and the temple where Ismenus
gives oracles by fire. King, you yourself
have seen our city reeling like a wreck
already; it can scarcely lift its prow

out of the depths, out of the bloody surf.
25 A blight is on the fruitful plants of the earth,
a blight is on the cattle in the fields,
a blight is on our women that no children
are born to them; a God that carries fire,
a deadly pestilence, is on our town,
strikes us and spares not, and the house of Cadmus
is emptied of its people while black Death
30 grows rich in groaning and in lamentation.
We have not come as suppliants to this altar
because we thought of you as of a God,
but rather judging you the first of men
in all the chances of this life and when
we mortals have to do with more than man.
35 You came and by your coming saved our city,
freed us from tribute which we paid of old
to the Sphinx, cruel singer. This you did
in virtue of no knowledge we could give you,
in virtue of no teaching; it was God
that aided you, men say, and you are held
with God's assistance to have saved our lives.
40 Now Oedipus, Greatest in all men's eyes,
here falling at your feet we all entreat you,
find us some strength for rescue.
Perhaps you'll hear a wise word from some God,
perhaps you will learn something from a man
(for I have seen that for the skilled of practice
45 the outcome of their counsels live the most).
Noblest of men, go, and raise up our city,
go,—and give heed. For now this land of ours
calls you its savior since you saved it once.
So, let us never speak about your reign
as of a time when first our feet were set
50 secure on high, but later fell to ruin.
Raise up our city, save it and raise it up.

Once you have brought us luck with happy omen;
be no less now in fortune.
If you will rule this land, as now you rule it,
better to rule it full of men than empty. 55
For neither tower nor ship is anything
when empty, and none live in it together.

OEDIPUS: I pity you, children. You have come full of
longing,
but I have known the story before you told it
only too well. I know you are all sick,
yet there is not one of you, sick though you are, 60
that is as sick as I myself.
Your several sorrows each have single scope
and touch but one of you. My spirit groans
for city and myself and you at once.
You have not roused me like a man from sleep; 65
know that I have given many tears to this,
gone many ways wandering in thought,
but as I thought I found only one remedy
and that I took. I sent Menoeceus' son
Creon, Jocasta's brother, to Apollo, 70
to his Pythian temple,
that he might learn there by what act or word
I could save this city. As I count the days,
it vexes me what ails him; he is gone
far longer than he needed for the journey. 75
But when he comes, then, may I prove a villain,
if I shall not do all the God commands.

PRIEST: Thanks for your gracious words. Your servants
here
signal that Creon is this moment coming.

OEDIPUS: His face is bright. O holy Lord Apollo, 80
grant that his news too may be bright for us
and bring us safety.

PRIEST: It is happy news,
    I think, for else his head would not be crowned
    with sprigs of fruitful laurel.

OEDIPUS: We will know soon,
85   he's within hail. Lord Creon, my good brother,
    what is the word you bring us from the God?
(*Creon enters.*)

CREON: A good word,—for things hard to bear
    themselves
    if in the final issue all is well
    I count complete good fortune.

OEDIPUS: What do you mean?
    What you have said so far
90   leaves me uncertain whether to trust or fear.

CREON: If you will hear my news before these others
    I am ready to speak, or else to go within.

OEDIPUS: Speak it to all;
    the grief I bear, I bear it more for these
    than for my own heart.

95   CREON: I will tell you, then,
    what I heard from the God.
    King Phoebus in plain words commanded us
    to drive out a pollution from our land,
    pollution grown ingrained within the land;
    drive it out, said the God, not cherish it,
    till it's past cure.

OEDIPUS: What is the rite
    of purification? How shall it be done?

100   CREON: By banishing a man, or expiation
    of blood by blood, since it is murder guilt
    which holds our city in this destroying storm.

OEDIPUS: Who is this man whose fate the God
   pronounces?

CREON: My Lord, before you piloted the state
   we had a king called Laius.

OEDIPUS: I know of him by hearsay. I have not seen him. 105

CREON: The God commanded clearly: let some one
   punish with force this dead man's murderers.

OEDIPUS: Where are they in the world? Where would a
   trace
   of this old crime be found? It would be hard
   to guess where.

CREON: The clue is in this land; 110
   that which is sought is found;
   the unheeded thing escapes:
   so said the God.

OEDIPUS: Was it at home,
   or in the country that death came upon him,
   or in another country traveling?

CREON: He went, he said himself, upon an embassy,
   but never returned when he set out from home. 115

OEDIPUS: Was there no messenger, no fellow traveler
   who knows what happened? Such a one might tell
   something of use.

CREON: They were all killed save one. He fled in terror
   and he could tell us nothing in clear terms
   of what he knew, nothing, but one thing only.

OEDIPUS: What was it? 120
   If we could even find a slim beginning
   in which to hope, we might discover much.

CREON: This man said that the robbers they encountered
    were many and the hands that did the murder
    were many; it was no man's single power.

OEDIPUS: How could a robber dare a deed like this
    were he not helped with money from the city,
125   money and treachery?

CREON: That indeed was thought.
    But Laius was dead and in our trouble
    there was none to help.

OEDIPUS: What trouble was so great to hinder you
    inquiring out the murder of your king?

130 CREON: The riddling Sphinx induced us to neglect
    mysterious crimes and rather seek solution
    of troubles at our feet.

OEDIPUS: I will bring this to light again. King Phoebus
    fittingly took this care about the dead,
    and you too fittingly.
135   And justly you will see in me an ally,
    a champion of my country and the God.
    For when I drive pollution from the land
    I will not serve a distant friend's advantage,
    but act in my own interest. Whoever
    he was that killed the king may readily
140   wish to dispatch me with his murderous hand;
    so helping the dead king I help myself.

    Come, children, take your suppliant boughs and go;
    up from the altars now. Call the assembly
    and let it meet upon the understanding
145   that I'll do everything. God will decide
    whether we prosper or remain in sorrow.

PRIEST: Rise, children—it was this we came to seek,
    which of himself the king now offers us.
    May Phoebus who gave us the oracle
    come to our rescue and stay the plague.   150
(*Exeunt all but the Chorus.*)

CHORUS
Strophe: What is the sweet spoken word of God from the
      shrine of Pytho rich in gold
    that has come to glorious Thebes?
    I am stretched on the rack of doubt, and terror and
      trembling hold
    my heart, O Delian Healer, and I worship full of fears
    for what doom you will bring to pass, new or renewed
      in the revolving years.   155
    Speak to me, immortal voice,
    child of golden Hope.

Antistrophe: First I call on you, Athene, deathless daughter
      of Zeus,
    and Artemis, Earth Upholder,   160
    who sits in the midst of the market place in the throne
      which men call Fame,
    and Phoebus, the Far Shooter, three averters of Fate,
    come to us now, if ever before, when ruin rushed upon
      the state,   165
    you drove destruction's flame away
    out of our land.

Strophe: Our sorrows defy number;
    all the ship's timbers are rotten;
    taking of thought is no spear for the driving away of the
      plague.   170
    There are no growing children in this famous land;
    there are no women bearing the pangs of childbirth.

175 You may see them one with another, like birds swift on
    the wing,
quicker than fire unmastered,
speeding away to the coast of the Western God.

Antistrophe: In the unnumbered deaths
of its people the city dies;
those children that are born lie dead on the naked earth
unpitied, spreading contagion of death; and gray haired
    mothers and wives
182–5 everywhere stand at the altar's edge, suppliant,
    moaning;
the hymn to the healing God rings out but with it the
    wailing voices are blended.
From these our sufferings grant us, O golden Daughter
    of Zeus,
glad-faced deliverance.

Strophe: There is no clash of brazen shields but our fight is
    with the War God,
191 a War God ringed with the cries of men, a savage God
    who burns us;
grant that he turn in racing course backwards out of our
    country's bounds
195 to the great palace of Amphitrite or where the waves of
    the Thracian sea
deny the stranger safe anchorage.
Whatsoever escapes the night
at last the light of day revisits;
so smite the War God, Father Zeus,
beneath your thunderbolt,
for you are the Lord of the lightning, the lightning that
200   carries fire.

Antistrophe: And your unconquered arrow shafts, winged
        by the golden corded bow,
    Lycean King, I beg to be at our side for help;   205
    and the gleaming torches of Artemis with which she
        scours the Lycean hills,
    and I call on the God with the turban of gold, who gave
        his name to this country of ours,   210
    the Bacchic God with the wind flushed face,
    Evian One, who travel
    with the Maenad company,
    combat the God that burns us
    with your torch of pine;
    for the God that is our enemy is a God unhonored   215
        among the Gods.
(*Oedipus returns.*)

OEDIPUS: For what you ask me—if you will hear my
        words,
    and hearing welcome them and fight the plague,
    you will find strength and lightening of your load.

    Hark to me; what I say to you, I say
    as one that is a stranger to the story
    as stranger to the deed. For I would not   220
    be far upon the track if I alone
    were tracing it without a clue. But now,
    since after all was finished, I became
    a citizen among you, citizens—
    now I proclaim to all the men of Thebes:
    who so among you knows the murderer   225
    by whose hand Laius, son of Labdacus,
    died—I command him to tell everything
    to me,—yes, though he fears himself to take the blame
    on his own head; for bitter punishment
    he shall have none, but leave this land unharmed.
    Or if he knows the murderer, another,   230

a foreigner, still let him speak the truth.
For I will pay him and be grateful, too.
But if you shall keep silence, if perhaps
some one of you, to shield a guilty friend,
or for his own sake shall reject my words—
235 hear what I shall do then:
I forbid that man, whoever he be, my land,
my land where I hold sovereignty and throne;
and I forbid any to welcome him
240 or cry him greeting or make him a sharer
in sacrifice or offering to the Gods,
or give him water for his hands to wash.
I command all to drive him from their homes,
since he is our pollution, as the oracle
of Pytho's God proclaimed him now to me.
So I stand forth a champion of the God
245 and of the man who died.
Upon the murderer I invoke this curse—
whether he is one man and all unknown,
or one of many—may he wear out his life
in misery to miserable doom!
250 If with my knowledge he lives at my hearth
I pray that I myself may feel my curse.
On you I lay my charge to fulfill all this
for me, for the God, and for this land of ours
destroyed and blighted, by God forsaken.

255 Even were this no matter of God's ordinance
it would not fit you so to leave it lie,
unpurified, since a good man is dead
and one that was a king. Search it out.
Since I am now the holder of his office,
260 and have his bed and wife that once was his,
and had his line not been unfortunate
we would have common children—(fortune leaped

upon his head)—because of all these things,
I fight in his defence as for my father,
and I shall try all means to take the murderer   265
of Laius the son of Labdacus
the son of Polydorus and before him
of Cadmus and before him of Agenor.
Those who do not obey me, may the Gods
grant no crops springing from the ground they plough   270
nor children to their women! May a fate
like this, or one still worse than this consume them!
For you whom these words please, the other Thebans,
may Justice as your ally and all the Gods
live with you, blessing you now and for ever!   275

CHORUS: As you have held me to my oath, I speak:
I neither killed the king nor can declare
the killer; but since Phoebus set the quest
it is his part to tell who the man is.

OEDIPUS: Right; but to put compulsion on the Gods   280
against their will—no man can do that.

CHORUS: May I then say what I think second best?

OEDIPUS: If there's a third best, too, spare not to tell it.

CHORUS: I know that what the Lord Teiresias
sees, is most often what the Lord Apollo   285
sees. If you should inquire of this from him
you might find out most clearly.

OEDIPUS: Even in this my actions have not been sluggard.
On Creon's word I have sent two messengers
and why the prophet is not here already
I have been wondering.

CHORUS: His skill apart   290
there is besides only an old faint story.

OEDIPUS: What is it?
I look at every story.

CHORUS: It was said
that he was killed by certain wayfarers.

OEDIPUS: I heard that, too, but no one saw the killer.

CHORUS: Yet if he has a share of fear at all,
295   his courage will not stand firm, hearing your curse.

OEDIPUS: The man who in the doing did not shrink
will fear no word.

CHORUS: Here comes his prosecutor:
led by your men the godly prophet comes
in whom alone of mankind truth is native.
(*Enter Teiresias, led by a little boy.*)

300   OEDIPUS: Teiresias, you are versed in everything,
things teachable and things not to be spoken,
things of the heaven and earth-creeping things.
You have no eyes but in your mind you know
with what a plague our city is afflicted.
My lord, in you alone we find a champion,
in you alone one that can rescue us.
305   Perhaps you have not heard the messengers,
but Phoebus sent in answer to our sending
an oracle declaring that our freedom
from this disease would only come when we
should learn the names of those who killed King Laius,
and kill them or expel from our country.
310   Do not begrudge us oracles from birds,
or any other way of prophecy
within your skill; save yourself and the city,
save me; redeem the debt of our pollution
that lies on us because of this dead man.
We are in your hands; pains are most nobly taken
315   to help another when you have means and power.

TEIRESIAS: Alas, how terrible is wisdom when
it brings no profit to the man that's wise!
This I knew well, but had forgotten it,
else I would not have come here.

OEDIPUS: What is this?
How sad you are now you have come!

TEIRESIAS: Let me
go home. It will be easiest for us both   320
to bear our several destinies to the end
if you will follow my advice.

OEDIPUS: You'd rob us
of this your gift of prophecy? You talk
as one who had no care for law nor love
for Thebes who reared you.

TEIRESIAS: Yes, but I see that even your own words
miss the mark; therefore I must fear for mine.   325

OEDIPUS: For God's sake if you know of anything,
do not turn from us; all of us kneel to you,
all of us here, your suppliants.

TEIRESIAS: All of you here know nothing. I will not
bring to the light of day my troubles, mine—
rather than call them yours.

OEDIPUS: What do you mean?
You know of something but refuse to speak.   330
Would you betray us and destroy the city?

TEIRESIAS: I will not bring this pain upon us both,
neither on you nor on myself. Why is it
you question me and waste your labor? I
will tell you nothing.

335 OEDIPUS: You would provoke a stone! Tell us, you villain,
tell us, and do not stand there quietly
unmoved and balking at the issue.

TEIRESIAS: You blame my temper but you do not see
your own that lives within you; it is me
you chide.

OEDIPUS: Who would not feel his temper rise
340 at words like these with which you shame our city?

TEIRESIAS: Of themselves things will come, although I
hide them
and breathe no word of them.

OEDIPUS: Since they will come
tell them to me.

TEIRESIAS: I will say nothing further.
Against this answer let your temper rage
as wildly as you will.

345 OEDIPUS: Indeed I am
so angry I shall not hold back a jot
of what I think. For I would have you know
I think you were complotter of the deed
and doer of the deed save in so far
as for the actual killing. Had you had eyes
I would have said alone you murdered him.

350 TEIRESIAS: Yes? Then I warn you faithfully to keep
the letter of your proclamation and
from this day forth to speak no word of greeting
to these nor me; you are the land's pollution.

OEDIPUS: How shamelessly you started up this taunt!
355 How do you think you will escape?

TEIRESIAS: I have.
  I have escaped; the truth is what I cherish
  and that's my strength.

OEDIPUS: And who has taught you truth?
  Not your profession surely!

TEIRESIAS: You have taught me,
  for you have made me speak against my will.

OEDIPUS: Speak what? Tell me again that I may learn it
      better.

TEIRESIAS: Did you not understand before or would you
      provoke me into speaking?   360

OEDIPUS: I did not grasp it,
  not so to call it known. Say it again.

TEIRESIAS: I say you are the murderer of the king
  whose murderer you seek.

OEDIPUS: Not twice you shall
  say calumnies like this and stay unpunished.

TEIRESIAS: Shall I say more to tempt your anger more?

OEDIPUS: As much as you desire; it will be said   365
  in vain.

TEIRESIAS: I say that with those you love best
  you live in foulest shame unconsciously
  and do not see where you are in calamity.

OEDIPUS: Do you imagine you can always talk
  like this, and live to laugh at it hereafter?

TEIRESIAS: Yes, if the truth has anything of strength.

OEDIPUS: It has, but not for you; it has no strength   370
  for you because you are blind in mind and ears
  as well as in your eyes.

TEIRESIAS: You are a poor wretch
   to taunt me with the very insults which
   every one soon will heap upon yourself.

OEDIPUS: Your life is one long night so that you cannot
375   hurt me or any other who sees the light.

TEIRESIAS: It is not fate that I should be your ruin,
   Apollo is enough; it is his care
   to work this out.

OEDIPUS: Was this your own design
   or Creon's?

TEIRESIAS: Creon is no hurt to you,
   but you are to yourself.

380 OEDIPUS: Wealth, sovereignty and skill outmatching skill
   for the contrivance of an envied life!
   Great store of jealousy fill your treasury chests,
385   if my friend Creon, friend from the first and loyal,
   'thus secretly attacks me, secretly
   desires to drive me out and secretly
   suborns this juggling, trick devising quack,
   this wily beggar who has only eyes
   for his own gains, but blindness in his skill.
390   For, tell me, where have you seen clear, Teiresias,
   with your prophetic eyes? When the dark singer,
   the Sphinx, was in your country, did you speak
   word of deliverance to its citizens?
   And yet the riddle's answer was not the province
   of a chance comer. It was a prophet's task
395   and plainly you had no such gift of prophecy
   from birds nor otherwise from any God
   to glean a word of knowledge. But I came,
   Oedipus, who knew nothing, and I stopped her.
   I solved the riddle by my wit alone.

Mine was no knowledge got from birds. And now
you would expel me,
because you think that you will find a place   400
by Creon's throne. I think you will be sorry,
both you and your accomplice, for your plot
to drive me out. And did I not regard you
as an old man, some suffering would have taught you
that what was in your heart was treason.

CHORUS: We look at this man's words and yours, my king,
and we find both have spoken them in anger.   405
We need no angry words but only thought
how we may best hit the God's meaning for us.

TEIRESIAS: If you are king, at least I have the right
no less to speak in my defense against you.
Of that much I am master. I am no slave   410
of yours, but Loxias', and so I shall not
enroll myself with Creon for my patron.
Since you have taunted me with being blind,
here is my word for you.
You have your eyes but see not where you are
in sin, nor where you live, nor whom you live with.
Do you know who your parents are? Unknowing   415
you are an enemy to kith and kin
in death, beneath the earth, and in this life.
A deadly footed, double striking curse,
from father and mother both, shall drive you forth
out of this land, with darkness on your eyes,
that now have such straight vision. Shall there be
a place will not be harbor to your cries,   420
a corner of Cithaeron will not ring
in echo to your cries, soon, soon,—
when you shall learn the secret of your marriage,
which steered you to a haven in this house,—
haven no haven, after lucky voyage?

And of the multitude of other evils
establishing a grim equality
425   between you and your children, you know nothing.
So, muddy with contempt my words and Creon's!
Misery shall grind no man as it will you.

OEDIPUS: Is it endurable that I should hear
430   such words from him? Go and a curse go with you!
Quick, home with you! Out of my house at once!

TEIRESIAS: I would not have come either had you not
called me.

OEDIPUS: I did not know then you would talk like a
fool—
or it would have been long before I called you.

435   TEIRESIAS: I am a fool then, as it seems to you—
but to the parents who have bred you, wise.

OEDIPUS: What parents? Stop! Who are they of all the
world?

TEIRESIAS: This day will show your birth and will destroy
you.

OEDIPUS: How needlessly your riddles darken everything.

440   TEIRESIAS: But it's in riddle answering you are strongest.

OEDIPUS: Yes. Taunt me where you will find me great.

TEIRESIAS: It is this very luck that has destroyed you.

OEDIPUS: I do not care, if it has saved this city.

TEIRESIAS: Well, I will go. Come, boy, lead me away.

445   OEDIPUS: Yes, lead him off. So long as you are here,
you'll be a stumbling block and a vexation;
once gone, you will not trouble me again.

TEIRESIAS: I have said
   what I came here to say not fearing your
   countenance: there is no way you can hurt me.
   I tell you, king, this man, this murderer
   (whom you have long declared you are in search of,
   indicting him in threatening proclamation   450
   as murderer of Laius)—he is here.
   In name he is a stranger among citizens
   but soon he will be shown to be a citizen
   true native Theban, and he'll have no joy
   of the discovery: blindness for sight
   and beggary for riches his exchange,   455
   he shall go journeying to a foreign country
   tapping his way before him with a stick.
   He shall be proved father and brother both
   to his own children in his house; to her
   that gave him birth, a son and husband both;
   a fellow sower in his father's bed
   with that same father that he murdered.
   Go within, reckon that out, and if you find me   460
   mistaken, say I have no skill in prophecy.
(*Exeunt separately Teiresias and Oedipus.*)

CHORUS
Strophe: Who is the man proclaimed
   by Delphi's prophetic rock
   as the bloody handed murderer,   465
   the doer of deeds that none dare name?
   Now is the time for him to run
   with a stronger foot
   than Pegasus
   for the child of Zeus leaps in arms upon him   470
   with fire and the lightning bolt,
   and terribly close on his heels
   are the Fates that never miss.

Antistrophe: Lately from snowy Parnassus
    clearly the voice flashed forth,
475   bidding each Theban track him down,
    the unknown murderer.
    In the savage forests he lurks and in
    the caverns like
    the mountain bull.
    He is sad and lonely, and lonely his feet
480   that carry him far from the navel of earth;
    but its prophecies, ever living,
    flutter around his head.

Strophe: The augur has spread confusion,
    terrible confusion;
485   I do not approve what was said
    nor can I deny it.
    I do not know what to say;
    I am in a flutter of foreboding;
    I never heard in the present
490   nor past of a quarrel between
    the sons of Labdacus and Polybus,
    that I might bring as proof
    in attacking the popular fame
    of Oedipus, seeking
    to take vengeance for undiscovered
495   death in the line of Labdacus.

Antistrophe: Truly Zeus and Apollo are wise
    and in human things all knowing;
500   but amongst men there is no
    distinct judgment, between the prophet
    and me—which of us is right.
    One man may pass another in wisdom
    but I would never agree
    with those that find fault with the king
    till I should see the word

proved right beyond doubt. For once
in visible form the Sphinx
came on him and all of us
saw his wisdom and in that test
he saved the city. So he will not be condemned by my
   mind.   512
(*Enter Creon.*)

CREON: Citizens, I have come because I heard
   deadly words spread about me, that the king
   accuses me. I cannot take that from him.
   If he believes that in these present troubles   515
   he has been wronged by me in word or deed
   I do not want to live on with the burden
   of such a scandal on me. The report   520
   injures me doubly and most vitally—
   for I'll be called a traitor to my city
   and traitor also to my friends and you.

CHORUS: Perhaps it was a sudden gust of anger
   that forced that insult from him, and no judgment.

CREON: But did he say that it was in compliance   525
   with schemes of mine that the seer told him lies?

CHORUS: Yes, he said that, but why, I do not know.

CREON: Were his eyes straight in his head? Was his mind
    right
   when he accused me in this fashion?

CHORUS: I do not know; I have no eyes to see   530
   what princes do. Here comes the king himself.
(*Enter Oedipus.*)

OEDIPUS: You, sir, how is it you come here? Have you so
    much
   brazen-faced daring that you venture in

my house although you are proved manifestly
the murderer of that man, and though you tried,
535   openly, highway robbery of my crown?
For God's sake, tell me what you saw in me,
what cowardice or what stupidity,
that made you lay a plot like this against me?
Did you imagine I should not observe
the crafty scheme that stole upon me or
540   seeing it, take no means to counter it?
Was it not stupid of you to make the attempt,
to try to hunt down royal power without
the people at your back or friends? For only
with the people at your back or money can
the hunt end in the capture of a crown.

CREON: Do you know what you're doing? Will you listen
to words to answer yours, and then pass judgment?

OEDIPUS: You're quick to speak, but I am slow to grasp
545   you,
for I have found you dangerous,—and my foe.

CREON: First of all hear what I shall say to that.

OEDIPUS: At least don't tell me that you are not guilty.

CREON: If you think obstinacy without wisdom
550   a valuable possession, you are wrong.

OEDIPUS: And you are wrong if you believe that one,
a criminal, will not be punished only
because he is my kinsman.

CREON: This is but just—
but tell me, then, of what offense I'm guilty?

555   OEDIPUS: Did you or did you not urge me to send
to this prophetic mumbler?

CREON: I did indeed,
  and I shall stand by what I told you.

OEDIPUS: How long ago is it since Laius. ...

CREON: What about Laius? I don't understand.

OEDIPUS: Vanished—died—was murdered?   560

CREON: It is long,
  a long, long time to reckon.

OEDIPUS: Was this prophet
  in the profession then?

CREON: He was, and honored
  as highly as he is today.

OEDIPUS: At that time did he say a word about me?

CREON: Never, at least when I was near him.   565

OEDIPUS: You never made a search for the dead man?

CREON: We searched, indeed, but never learned of
      anything.

OEDIPUS: Why did our wise old friend not say this then?

CREON: I don't know; and when I know nothing, I
  usually hold my tongue.

OEDIPUS: You know this much,   570
  and can declare this much if you are loyal.

CREON: What is it? If I know, I'll not deny it.

OEDIPUS: That he would not have said that I killed Laius
  had he not met you first.

CREON: You know yourself
  whether he said this, but I demand that I   575
  should hear as much from you as you from me.

OEDIPUS: Then hear,—I'll not be proved a murderer.

CREON: Well, then. You're married to my sister.

OEDIPUS: Yes,
that I am not disposed to deny.

CREON: You rule
this country giving her an equal share
in the government?

580   OEDIPUS: Yes, everything she wants
she has from me.

CREON: And I, as thirdsman to you,
am rated as the equal of you two?

OEDIPUS: Yes, and it's there you've proved yourself false
    friend.

CREON: Not if you will reflect on it as I do.
    Consider, first, if you think any one
585   would choose to rule and fear rather than rule
    and sleep untroubled by a fear if power
    were equal in both cases. I, at least,
    I was not born with such a frantic yearning
    to be a king—but to do what kings do.
    And so it is with every one who has learned
    wisdom and self-control. As it stands now,
590   the prizes are all mine—and without fear.
    But if I were the king myself, I must
    do much that went against the grain.
    How should despotic rule seem sweeter to me
    than painless power and an assured authority?
    I am not so besotted yet that I
595   want other honors than those that come with profit.
    Now every man's my pleasure; every man greets me;
    now those who are your suitors fawn on me,—

success for them depends upon my favor.
Why should I let all this go to win that?
My mind would not be traitor if it's wise;   600
I am no treason lover, of my nature,
nor would I ever dare to join a plot.
Prove what I say. Go to the oracle
at Pytho and inquire about the answers,
if they are as I told you. For the rest,   605
if you discover I laid any plot
together with the seer, kill me, I say,
not only by your vote but by my own.
But do not charge me on obscure opinion
without some proof to back it. It's not just
lightly to count your knaves as honest men,   610
nor honest men as knaves. To throw away
an honest friend is, as it were, to throw
your life away, which a man loves the best.
In time you will know all with certainty;
time is the only test of honest men,
one day is space enough to know a rogue.   615

CHORUS: His words are wise, king, if one fears to fall.
    Those who are quick of temper are not safe.

OEDIPUS: When he that plots against me secretly
    moves quickly, I must quickly counterplot.
    If I wait taking no decisive measure   620
    his business will be done, and mine be spoiled.

CREON: What do you want to do then? Banish me?

OEDIPUS: No, certainly; kill you, not banish you.[1]

    1. Two lines omitted here owing to the confusion in the dialogue
consequent on the loss of a third line. The lines as they stand in Jebb's
edition (1902) are:
OED.: That you may show what manner of thing is envy.
CREON: You speak as one that will not yield or trust.
[OED. lost line.]

626   CREON: I do not think that you've your wits about you.

OEDIPUS: For my own interests, yes.

CREON: But for mine, too,
  you should think equally.

OEDIPUS: You are a rogue.

CREON: Suppose you do not understand?

OEDIPUS: But yet
  I must be ruler.

CREON: Not if you rule badly.

OEDIPUS: O, city! city!

630   CREON: I too have some share
  in the city; it is not yours alone.

CHORUS: Stop, my lords! Here—and in the nick of time
  I see Jocasta coming from the house;
  with her help lay the quarrel that now stirs you.
(*Enter Jocasta.*)

JOCASTA: For shame! Why have you raised this foolish
    squabbling
635   brawl? Are you not ashamed to air your private
  griefs when the country's sick? Go in, you, Oedipus,
  and you, too, Creon, into the house. Don't magnify
  your nothing troubles.

CREON: Sister, Oedipus,
  your husband, thinks he has the right to do
640   terrible wrongs—he has but to choose between
  two terrors: banishing or killing me.

OEDIPUS: He's right, Jocasta; for I find him plotting
  with knavish tricks against my person.

CREON: That God may never bless me! May I die
   accursed, if I have been guilty of   645
   one tittle of the charge you bring against me!

JOCASTA: I beg you, Oedipus, trust him in this,
   spare him for the sake of this his oath to God,
   for my sake, and the sake of those who stand here.

CHORUS: Be gracious, be merciful,   649
   we beg of you.

OEDIPUS: In what would you have me yield?

CHORUS: He has been no silly child in the past.
   He is strong in his oath now.
   Spare him.

OEDIPUS: Do you know what you ask?

CHORUS: Yes.

OEDIPUS: Tell me then.

CHORUS: He has been your friend before all men's eyes; do 656
   not cast him away dishonored on an obscure conjecture.

OEDIPUS: I would have you know that this request of
     yours
   really requests my death or banishment.

CHORUS: May the Sun God, king of Gods, forbid! May I   660
   die without God's blessing, without friends' help, if I
   had any such thought. But my spirit is broken by my
   unhappiness for my wasting country; and this would   665
   but add troubles amongst ourselves to the other troubles.

OEDIPUS: Well, let him go then—if I must die ten times
     for it,   669
   or be sent out dishonored into exile.
   It is your lips that prayed for him I pitied,
   not his; wherever he is, I shall hate him.

CREON: I see you sulk in yielding and you're dangerous
　　　when you are out of temper; natures like yours
675　　are justly heaviest for themselves to bear.

OEDIPUS: Leave me alone! Take yourself off, I tell you.

CREON: I'll go, you have not known me, but they have,
　　　and they have known my innocence.
(*Exit*.)

CHORUS: Won't you take him inside, lady?

680 JOCASTA: Yes, when I've found out what was the matter.

CHORUS: There was some misconceived suspicion of a
　　　story, and on the other side the sting of injustice.

JOCASTA: So, on both sides?

CHORUS: Yes.

JOCASTA: What was the story?

685 CHORUS: I think it best, in the interests of the country, to
　　　leave it where it ended.

OEDIPUS: You see where you have ended, straight of
　　　judgment
　　　although you are, by softening my anger.

689 CHORUS: Sir, I have said before and I say again—be sure
　　　that I would have been proved a madman, bankrupt in
　　　sane counsel, if I should put you away, you who steered
　　　the country I love safely when she was crazed with
695　　troubles. God grant that now, too, you may prove a
　　　fortunate guide for us.

JOCASTA: Tell me, my lord, I beg of you, what was it
　　　that roused your anger so?

OEDIPUS: Yes, I will tell you.   700
   I honor you more than I honor them.
   It was Creon and the plots he laid against me.

JOCASTA: Tell me—if you can clearly tell the quarrel—

OEDIPUS: Creon says
   that I'm the murderer of Laius.

JOCASTA: Of his own knowledge or on information?

OEDIPUS: He sent this rascal prophet to me, since   705
   he keeps his own mouth clean of any guilt.

JOCASTA: Do not concern yourself about this matter;
   listen to me and learn that human beings
   have no part in the craft of prophecy.
   Of that I'll show you a short proof.   710
   There was an oracle once that came to Laius,—
   I will not say that it was Phoebus' own,
   but it was from his servants—and it told him
   that it was fate that he should die a victim
   at the hands of his own son, a son to be born
   of Laius and me. But, see now, he,
   the king, was killed by foreign highway robbers   715
   at a place where three roads meet—so goes the story;
   and for the son—before three days were out
   after his birth King Laius pierced his ankles
   and by the hands of others cast him forth
   upon a pathless hillside. So Apollo   720
   failed to fulfill his oracle to the son,
   that he should kill his father, and to Laius
   also proved false in that the thing he feared,
   death at his son's hands, never came to pass.
   So clear in this case were the oracles,
   so clear and false. Give them no heed, I say;
   what God discovers need of, easily
   he shows to us himself.   725

OEDIPUS: O dear Jocasta,
as I hear this from you, there comes upon me
a wandering of the soul—I could run mad.

JOCASTA: What trouble is it, that you turn again
and speak like this?

OEDIPUS: I thought I heard you say
730   that Laius was killed at a crossroads.

JOCASTA: Yes, that was how the story went and still
that word goes round.

OEDIPUS: Where is this place, Jocasta,
where he was murdered?

JOCASTA: Phocis is the country
and the road splits there, one of two roads from Delphi,
another comes from Daulia.

735   OEDIPUS: How long ago is this?

JOCASTA: The news came to the city just before
you became king and all men's eyes looked to you.
What is it, Oedipus, that's in your mind?

OEDIPUS: What have you designed, O Zeus, to do with
       me?

JOCASTA: What is the thought that troubles your heart?

740   OEDIPUS: Don't ask me yet—tell me of Laius—
How did he look? How old or young was he?

JOCASTA: He was a tall man and his hair was grizzled
already—nearly white—and in his form
not unlike you.

OEDIPUS: O God, I think I have
745   called curses on myself in ignorance.

JOCASTA: What do you mean? I am terrified
    when I look at you.

OEDIPUS: I have a deadly fear
    that the old seer had eyes. You'll show me more
    if you can tell me one more thing.

JOCASTA: I will.
    I'm frightened,—but if I can understand,
    I'll tell you all you ask.

OEDIPUS: How was his company?   750
    Had he few with him when he went this journey,
    or many servants, as would suit a prince?

JOCASTA: In all there were but five, and among them
    a herald; and one carriage for the king.

OEDIPUS: It's plain—it's plain—who was it told you this?   755

JOCASTA: The only servant that escaped safe home.

OEDIPUS: Is he at home now?

JOCASTA: No, when he came home again
    and saw you king and Laius was dead,
    he came to me and touched my hand and begged   760
    that I should send him to the fields to be
    my shepherd and so he might see the city
    as far off as he might. So I
    sent him away. He was an honest man,
    as slaves go, and was worthy of far more
    than what he asked of me.

OEDIPUS: O, how I wish that he could come back quickly!   765

JOCASTA: He can. Why is your heart so set on this?

OEDIPUS: O dear Jocasta, I am full of fears
    that I have spoken far too much; and therefore
    I wish to see this shepherd.

JOCASTA: He will come;
   but, Oedipus, I think I'm worthy too
770   to know what it is that disquiets you.

OEDIPUS: It shall not be kept from you, since my mind
   has gone so far with its forebodings. Whom
   should I confide in rather than you, who is there
   of more importance to me who have passed
   through such a fortune?
   Polybus was my father, king of Corinth,
775   and Merope, the Dorian, my mother.
   I was held greatest of the citizens
   in Corinth till a curious chance befell me
   as I shall tell you—curious, indeed,
   but hardly worth the store I set upon it.
   There was a dinner and at it a man,
780   a drunken man, accused me in his drink
   of being bastard. I was furious
   but held my temper under for that day.
   Next day I went and taxed my parents with it;
   they took the insult very ill from him,
   the drunken fellow who had uttered it.
785   So I was comforted for their part, but
   still this thing rankled always, for the story
   crept about widely. And I went at last
   to Pytho, though my parents did not know.
   But Phoebus sent me home again unhonored
790   in what I came to learn, but he foretold
   other and desperate horrors to befall me,
   that I was fated to lie with my mother,
   and show to daylight an accursed breed
   which men would not endure, and I was doomed
   to be murderer of the father that begot me.
   When I heard this I fled, and in the days
795   that followed I would measure from the stars

the whereabouts of Corinth—yes, I fled
to somewhere where I should not see fulfilled
the infamies told in that dreadful oracle.
And as I journeyed I came to the place
where, as you say, this king met with his death.
Jocasta, I will tell you the whole truth. 800
When I was near the branching of the crossroads,
going on foot, I was encountered by
a herald and a carriage with a man in it,
just as you tell me. He that led the way
and the old man himself wanted to thrust me 805
out of the road by force. I became angry
and struck the coachman who was pushing me.
When the old man saw this he watched his moment,
and as I passed he struck me from his carriage,
full on the head with his two pointed goad.
But he was paid in full and presently 810
my stick had struck him backwards from the car
and he rolled out of it. And then I killed them
all. If it happened there was any tie
of kinship twixt this man and Laius,
who is then now more miserable than I, 815
what man on earth so hated by the Gods,
since neither citizen nor foreigner
may welcome me at home or even greet me,
but drive me out of doors? And it is I,
I and no other have so cursed myself. 820
And I pollute the bed of him I killed
by the hands that killed him. Was I not born evil?
Am I not utterly unclean? I had to fly
and in my banishment not even see
my kindred nor set foot in my own country,
or otherwise my fate was to be yoked 825
in marriage with my mother and kill my father,
Polybus who begot me and had reared me.

Would not one rightly judge and say that on me
these things were sent by some malignant God?
830   O no, no, no—O holy majesty
of God on high, may I not see that day!
May I be gone out of men's sight before
I see the deadly taint of this disaster
come upon me.

CHORUS: Sir, we too fear these things. But until you see
835   this man face to face and hear his story, hope.

OEDIPUS: Yes, I have just this much of hope—to wait until
the herdsman comes.

JOCASTA: And when he comes, what do you want with
him?

OEDIPUS: I'll tell you; if I find that his story is the same as
840   yours, I at least will be clear of this guilt.

JOCASTA: Why, what so particularly did you learn from
my story?

OEDIPUS: You said that he spoke of highway *robbers* who
killed Laius. Now if he uses the same number, it was not
845   I who killed him. One man cannot be the same as many.
But if he speaks of a man traveling alone, then clearly
the burden of the guilt inclines towards me.

JOCASTA: Be sure, at least, that this was how he told the
850   story. He cannot unsay it now, for every one in the city
heard it—not I alone. But, Oedipus, even if he diverges
from what he said then, he shall never prove that the
murder of Laius squares rightly with the prophecy—
for Loxias declared that the king should be killed by
855   his own son. And that poor creature did not kill him
surely,—for he died himself first. So as far as prophecy
goes, henceforward I shall not look to the right hand or
the left.

OEDIPUS: Right. But yet, send some one for the peasant to   860
  bring him here; do not neglect it.

JOCASTA: I will send quickly. Now let me go indoors. I
  will do nothing except what pleases you.
(*Exeunt.*)

CHORUS
Strophe: May destiny ever find me
  pious in word and deed   865
  prescribed by the laws that live on high:
  laws begotten in the clear air of heaven,
  whose only father is Olympus;
  no mortal nature brought them to birth,
  no forgetfulness shall lull them to sleep;   870
  for God is great in them and grows not old.

Antistrophe: Insolence breeds the tyrant, insolence
  if it is glutted with a surfeit, unseasonable, unprofitable,   875
  climbs to the roof-top and plunges
  sheer down to the ruin that must be,
  and there its feet are no service.
  But I pray that the God may never   880
  abolish the eager ambition that profits the state.
  For I shall never cease to hold the God as our protector.

Strophe: If a man walks with haughtiness
  of hand or word and gives no heed   885
  to Justice and the shrines of Gods
  despises—may an evil doom
  smite him for his ill-starred pride of heart!—
  if he reaps gains without justice
  and will not hold from impiety   890
  and his fingers itch for untouchable things.
  When such things are done, what man shall contrive
  to shield his soul from the shafts of the God?
  When such deeds are held in honor,   895
  why should I honor the Gods in the dance?

Antistrophe: No longer to the holy place,
    to the navel of earth I'll go
    to worship, nor to Abae
900   nor to Olympia,
    unless the oracles are proved to fit,
    for all men's hands to point at.
    O Zeus, if you are rightly called
    the sovereign lord, all-mastering,
905   let this not escape you nor your ever-living power!
    The oracles concerning Laius
    are old and dim and men regard them not.
    Apollo is nowhere clear in honor; God's service
910   perishes.
  (*Enter Jocasta, carrying garlands.*)

JOCASTA: Princes of the land, I have had the thought to go
    to the Gods' temples, bringing in my hand
    garlands and gifts of incense, as you see.
    For Oedipus excites himself too much
915   at every sort of trouble, not conjecturing,
    like a man of sense, what will be from what was,
    but he is always at the speaker's mercy,
    when he speaks terrors. I can do no good
    by my advice, and so I came as suppliant
    to you, Lycaean Apollo, who are nearest.
920   These are the symbols of my prayer and this
    my prayer: grant us escape free of the curse.
    Now when we look to him we are all afraid;
    he's pilot of our ship and he is frightened.
  (*Enter Messenger.*)

925 MESSENGER: Might I learn from you, sirs, where is the
    house of Oedipus? Or best of all, if you know, where is
    the king himself?

CHORUS: This is his house and he is within doors. This
    lady is his wife and mother of his children.

MESSENGER: God bless you, lady, and God bless your   930
   household! God bless Oedipus' noble wife!

JOCASTA: God bless you, sir, for your kind greeting! What
   do you want of us that you have come here? What
   have you to tell us?

MESSENGER: Good news, lady. Good for your house and
   for your husband.

JOCASTA: What is your news? Who sent you to us?   935

MESSENGER: I come from Corinth and the news I bring
   will give you pleasure. Perhaps a little pain too.

JOCASTA: What is this news of double meaning?

MESSENGER: The people of the Isthmus will choose   940
   Oedipus to be their king. That is the rumour there.

JOCASTA: But isn't their king still old Polybus?

MESSENGER: No. He is in his grave. Death has got him.

JOCASTA: Is that the truth? Is Oedipus' father dead?

MESSENGER: May I die myself if it be otherwise!

JOCASTA: (*to a servant*) Be quick and run to the King with   945
   the news! O oracles of the Gods, where are you now? It
   was from this man Oedipus fled, lest he should be his
   murderer! And now he is dead, in the course of nature,
   and not killed by Oedipus.
(*Enter Oedipus.*)

OEDIPUS: Dearest Jocasta, why have you sent for me?   950

JOCASTA: Listen to this man and when you hear reflect
   what is the outcome of the holy oracles of the Gods.

OEDIPUS: Who is he? What is his message for me?

955 JOCASTA: He is from Corinth and he tells us that your
      father Polybus is dead and gone.

OEDIPUS: What's this you say, sir? Tell me yourself.

MESSENGER: Since this is the first matter you want clearly
      told: Polybus has gone down to death. You may be
      sure of it.

960 OEDIPUS: By treachery or sickness?

MESSENGER: A small thing will put old bodies asleep.

OEDIPUS: So he died of sickness, it seems—poor old man!

MESSENGER: Yes, and of age—the long years he had
      measured.

OEDIPUS: Ha! Ha! O dear Jocasta, why should one
965   look to the Pythian hearth? Why should one look
    to the birds screaming overhead? They prophesied
    that I should kill my father! But he's dead,
    and hidden deep in earth, and I stand here
    who never laid a hand on spear against him,—
    unless perhaps he died of longing for me,
970   and thus I am his murderer. But they,
    the oracles, as they stand—he's taken them
    away with him, they're dead as he himself is
    and worthless.

JOCASTA: That I told you before now.

OEDIPUS: You did, but I was misled by my fear.

975 JOCASTA: Then lay no more of them to heart, not one.

OEDIPUS: But surely I must fear my mother's bed?

JOCASTA: Why should man fear since chance is all in all
      for him, and he can clearly foreknow nothing?
      Best to live lightly, as one can, unthinkingly.

As to your mother's marriage bed,—don't fear it.   980
Before this, in dreams too, as well as oracles,
many a man has lain with his own mother.
But he to whom such things are nothing bears
his life most easily.

OEDIPUS: All that you say would be said perfectly
if she were dead; but since she lives I must   985
still fear, although you talk so well, Jocasta.

JOCASTA: Still in your father's death there's light of
comfort?

OEDIPUS: Great light of comfort; but I fear the living.

MESSENGER: Who is the woman that makes you afraid?

OEDIPUS: Merope, old man, Polybus' wife.   990

MESSENGER: What about her frightens the queen and you?

OEDIPUS: A terrible oracle, stranger, from the Gods.

MESSENGER: Can it be told? Or does the sacred law
forbid another to have knowledge of it?

OEDIPUS: O no! Once on a time Loxias said
that I should lie with my own mother and   995
take on my hands the blood of my own father.
And so for these long years I've lived away
from Corinth; it has been to my great happiness;
but yet it's sweet to see the face of parents.

MESSENGER: This was the fear which drove you out of
Corinth?   1000

OEDIPUS: Old man, I did not wish to kill my father.

MESSENGER: Why should I not free you from this fear, sir,
since I have come to you in all goodwill?

OEDIPUS: You would not find me thankless if you did.

MESSENGER: Why, it was just for this I brought the
1005   news,—
         to earn your thanks when you had come safe home.

OEDIPUS: No, I will never come near my parents.

MESSENGER: Son,
         it's very plain you don't know what you're doing.

OEDIPUS: What do you mean, old man? For God's sake,
         tell me.

MESSENGER: If your homecoming is checked by fears like
1010   these.

OEDIPUS: Yes, I'm afraid that Phoebus may prove right.

MESSENGER: The murder and the incest?

OEDIPUS: Yes, old man;
         that is my constant terror.

MESSENGER: Do you know
         that all your fears are empty?

1015 OEDIPUS: How is that,
         if they are father and mother and I their son?

MESSENGER: Because Polybus was no kin to you in blood.

OEDIPUS: What, was not Polybus my father?

MESSENGER: No more than I but just so much.

OEDIPUS: How can
         my father be my father as much as one
         that's nothing to me?

1020 MESSENGER: Neither he nor I
         begat you.

OEDIPUS: Why then did he call me son?

MESSENGER: A gift he took you from these hands of mine.

OEDIPUS: Did he love so much what he took from
another's hand?

MESSENGER: His childlessness before persuaded him.

OEDIPUS: Was I a child you bought or found when I   1025
was given to him?

MESSENGER: On Cithaeron's slopes
in the twisting thickets you were found.

OEDIPUS: And why
were you a traveler in those parts?

MESSENGER: I was
in charge of mountain flocks.

OEDIPUS: You were a shepherd?
A hireling vagrant?

MESSENGER: Yes, but at least at that time   1030
the man that saved your life, son.

OEDIPUS: What ailed me when you took me in your arms?

MESSENGER: In that your ankles should be witnesses.

OEDIPUS: Why do you speak of that old pain?

MESSENGER: I loosed you;
the tendons of your feet were pierced and fettered,—

OEDIPUS: My swaddling clothes brought me a rare
disgrace.   1035

MESSENGER: So that from this you're called your present
name.

OEDIPUS: Was this my father's doing or my mother's?
For God's sake, tell me.

MESSENGER: I don't know, but he
who gave you to me has more knowledge than I.

OEDIPUS: You yourself did not find me then? You took me
from someone else?

1040 MESSENGER: Yes, from another shepherd.

OEDIPUS: Who was he? Do you know him well enough
to tell?

MESSENGER: He was called Laius' man.

OEDIPUS: You mean the king who reigned here in the old
days?

MESSENGER: Yes, he was that man's shepherd.

1045 OEDIPUS: Is he alive
still, so that I could see him?

MESSENGER: You who live here
would know that best.

OEDIPUS: Do any of you here
know of this shepherd whom he speaks about
1050 in town or in the fields? Tell me. It's time
that this was found out once for all.

CHORUS: I think he is none other than the peasant
whom you have sought to see already; but
Jocasta here can tell us best of that.

OEDIPUS: Jocasta, do you know about this man
1055 whom we have sent for? Is he the man he mentions?

JOCASTA: Why ask of whom he spoke? Don't give it heed;
nor try to keep in mind what has been said.
It will be wasted labor.

OEDIPUS: With such clues
  I could not fail to bring my birth to light.

JOCASTA: I beg you—do not hunt this out—I beg you,   1060
  if you have any care for your own life.
  What I am suffering is enough.

OEDIPUS: Keep up
  your heart, Jocasta. Though I'm proved a slave,
  thrice slave, and though my mother is thrice slave,
  you'll not be shown to be of lowly lineage.

JOCASTA: O be persuaded by me, I entreat you;
  do not do this.

OEDIPUS: I will not be persuaded to let be   1065
  the chance of finding out the whole thing clearly.

JOCASTA: It is because I wish you well that I
  give you this counsel—and it's the best counsel.

OEDIPUS: Then the best counsel vexes me, and has
  for some while since.

JOCASTA: O Oedipus, God help you!
  God keep you from the knowledge of who you are!

OEDIPUS: Here, some one, go and fetch the shepherd for
    me;
  and let her find her joy in her rich family!   1070

JOCASTA: O Oedipus, unhappy Oedipus!
  that is all I can call you, and the last thing
  that I shall ever call you.
(*Exit.*)

CHORUS: Why has the queen gone, Oedipus, in wild
  grief rushing from us? I am afraid that trouble   1075
  will break out of this silence.

OEDIPUS: Break out what will! I at least shall be
    willing to see my ancestry, though humble.
    Perhaps she is ashamed of my low birth,
    for she has all a woman's high-flown pride.
1080   But I account myself a child of Fortune,
    beneficent Fortune, and I shall not be
    dishonored. She's the mother from whom I spring;
    the months, my brothers, marked me, now as small,
    and now again as mighty. Such is my breeding,
1085   and I shall never prove so false to it,
    as not to find the secret of my birth.

CHORUS
Strophe: If I am a prophet and wise of heart
1090   you shall not fail, Cithaeron,
    by the limitless sky, you shall not!—
    to know at tomorrow's full moon
    that Oedipus honors you,
    as native to him and mother and nurse at once;
    and that you are honored in dancing by us, as finding
        favor in sight of our king.
    Apollo, to whom we cry, find these things pleasing!

1098 *Antistrophe*: Who was it bore you, child? One of
    the long-lived nymphs who lay with Pan—
    the father who treads the hills?
    Or was she a bride of Loxias, your mother? The grassy
        slopes
1104   are all of them dear to him. Or perhaps Cyllene's king
    or the Bacchants' God that lives on the tops
    of the hills received you a gift from some
    one of the Helicon Nymphs, with whom he mostly
        plays?
(*Enter an old man, led by Oedipus' servants.*)

OEDIPUS: If some one like myself who never met him   1110
    may make a guess,—I think this is the herdsman,
    whom we were seeking. His old age is consonant
    with the other. And besides, the men who bring him
    I recognize as my own servants. You   1115
    perhaps may better me in knowledge since
    you've seen the man before.

CHORUS: You can be sure
    I recognize him. For if Laius
    had ever an honest shepherd, this was he.

OEDIPUS: You, sir, from Corinth, I must ask you first,
    is this the man you spoke of?   1120

MESSENGER: This is he
    before your eyes.

OEDIPUS: Old man, look here at me
    and tell me what I ask you. Were you ever
    a servant of King Laius?

HERDSMAN: I was,—
    no slave he bought but reared in his own house.

OEDIPUS: What did you do as work? How did you live?

HERDSMAN: Most of my life was spent among the flocks.   1125

OEDIPUS: In what part of the country did you live?

HERDSMAN: Cithaeron and the places near to it.

OEDIPUS: And somewhere there perhaps you knew this
    man?

HERDSMAN: What was his occupation? Who?

OEDIPUS: This man here,   1130
    have you had any dealings with him?

HERDSMAN: No—
not such that I can quickly call to mind.

MESSENGER: That is no wonder, master. But I'll make him
remember what he does not know. For I know, that he
1135   well knows the country of Cithaeron, how he with two
flocks, I with one kept company for three years—each
year half a year—from spring till autumn time and then
when winter came I drove my flocks to our fold home
1140   again and he to Laius' steadings. Well—am I right or
not in what I said we did?

HERDSMAN: You're right—although it's a long time ago.

MESSENGER: Do you remember giving me a child
to bring up as my foster child?

HERDSMAN: What's this?
Why do you ask this question?

1145   MESSENGER: Look old man,
here he is—here's the man who was that child!

HERDSMAN: Death take you! Won't you hold your tongue?

OEDIPUS: No, no,
do not find fault with him, old man. Your words
are more at fault than his.

HERDSMAN: O best of masters,
how do I give offense?

1150   OEDIPUS: When you refuse
to speak about the child of whom he asks you.

HERDSMAN: He speaks out of his ignorance, without
meaning.

OEDIPUS: If you'll not talk to gratify me, you
will talk with pain to urge you.

HERDSMAN: O please, sir,
don't hurt an old man, sir.

OEDIPUS: (*to the servants*) Here, one of you,
twist his hands behind him.

HERDSMAN: Why, God help me, why?   1155
What do you want to know?

OEDIPUS: You gave a child
to him,—the child he asked you of?

HERDSMAN: I did.
I wish I'd died the day I did.

OEDIPUS: You will
unless you tell me truly.

HERDSMAN: And I'll die
far worse if I should tell you.

OEDIPUS: This fellow   1160
is bent on more delays, as it would seem.

HERDSMAN: O no, no! I have told you that I gave it.

OEDIPUS: Where did you get this child from? Was it your
own or did you get it from another?

HERDSMAN: Not
my own at all; I had it from some one.

OEDIPUS: One of these citizens? or from what house?

HERDSMAN: O master, please—I beg you, master, please   1165
don't ask me more.

OEDIPUS: You're a dead man if I
ask you again.

HERDSMAN: It was one of the children
of Laius.

OEDIPUS: A slave? Or born in wedlock?

HERDSMAN: O God, I am on the brink of frightful speech.

1170 OEDIPUS: And I of frightful hearing. But I must hear.

HERDSMAN: The child was called his child; but she within,
  your wife would tell you best how all this was.

OEDIPUS: She gave it to you?

HERDSMAN: Yes, she did, my lord.

OEDIPUS: To do what with it?

HERDSMAN: Make away with it.

1175 OEDIPUS: She was so hard—its mother?

HERDSMAN: Aye, through fear
  of evil oracles.

OEDIPUS: Which?

HERDSMAN: They said that he
  should kill his parents.

OEDIPUS: How was it that you
  gave it away to this old man?

HERDSMAN: O master,
  I pitied it, and thought that I could send it
  off to another country and this man
1180 was from another country. But he saved it
  for the most terrible troubles. If you are
  the man he says you are, you're bred to misery.

OEDIPUS: O, O, O, they will all come,
  all come out clearly! Light of the sun, let me
  look upon you no more after today!
  I who first saw the light bred of a match
  accursed, and accursed in my living
1185 with them I lived with, cursed in my killing.
  (*Exeunt all but the Chorus.*)

CHORUS

Strophe: O generations of men, how I
   count you as equal with those who live
   not at all!
   What man, what man on earth wins more   1190
   of happiness than a seeming
   and after that turning away?
   Oedipus, you are my pattern of this,
   Oedipus, you and your fate!
   Luckless Oedipus, whom of all men   1196
   I envy not at all.

Antistrophe: In as much as he shot his bolt
   beyond the others and won the prize
   of happiness complete—
   O Zeus—and killed and reduced to nought
   the hooked taloned maid of the riddling speech,
   standing a tower against death for my land:
   hence he was called my king and hence
   was honored the highest of all
   honors; and hence he ruled
   in the great city of Thebes.

Strophe: But now whose tale is more miserable?   1204
   Who is there lives with a savager fate?
   Whose troubles so reverse his life as his?

   O Oedipus, the famous prince
   for whom a great haven
   the same both as father and son
   sufficed for generation,
   how, O how, have the furrows ploughed
   by your father endured to bear you, poor wretch,
   and hold their peace so long?

Antistrophe: Time who sees all has found you out   1213
   against your will; judges your marriage accursed,
   begetter and begot at one in it.

O child of Laius,
would I had never seen you.
I weep for you and cry
a dirge of lamentation.

To speak directly, I drew my breath
1222   from you at the first and so now I lull
my mouth to sleep with your name.
(*Enter a second messenger.*)

SECOND MESSENGER: O Princes always honored by our
      country,
what deeds you'll hear of and what horrors see,
1225   what grief you'll feel, if you as true born Thebans
care for the house of Labdacus's sons.
Phasis nor Ister cannot purge this house,
I think, with all their streams, such things
it hides, such evils shortly will bring forth
1230   into the light, whether they will or not;
and troubles hurt the most
when they prove self-inflicted.

CHORUS: What we had known before did not fall short
of bitter groaning's worth; what's more to tell?

SECOND MESSENGER: Shortest to hear and tell—our
1235   glorious queen
Jocasta's dead.

CHORUS: Unhappy woman! How?

SECOND MESSENGER: By her own hand. The worst of
      what was done
you cannot know. You did not see the sight.
Yet in so far as I remember it
1240   you'll hear the end of our unlucky queen.
When she came raging into the house she went
straight to her marriage bed, tearing her hair

with both her hands, and crying upon Laius   1245
long dead—Do you remember, Laius,
that night long past which bred a child for us
to send you to your death and leave
a mother making children with her son?
And then she groaned and cursed the bed in which
she brought forth husband by her husband, children   1250
by her own child, an infamous double bond.
How after that she died I do not know,—
for Oedipus distracted us from seeing.
He burst upon us shouting and we looked
to him as he paced frantically around,
begging us always: Give me a sword, I say,   1255
to find this wife no wife, this mother's womb,
this field of double sowing whence I sprang
and where I sowed my children! As he raved
some god showed him the way—none of us there.
Bellowing terribly and led by some   1260
invisible guide he rushed on the two doors,—
wrenching the hollow bolts out of their sockets,
he charged inside. There, there, we saw his wife
hanging, the twisted rope around her neck.
When he saw her, he cried out fearfully   1265
and cut the dangling noose. Then, as she lay,
poor woman, on the ground, what happened after,
was terrible to see. He tore the brooches—
the gold chased brooches fastening her robe—
away from her and lifting them up high
dashed them on his own eyeballs, shrieking out   1270
such things as: they will never see the crime
I have committed or had done upon me!
Dark eyes, now in the days to come look on
forbidden faces, do not recognize
those whom you long for—with such imprecations
he struck his eyes again and yet again   1275

with the brooches. And the bleeding eyeballs gushed
and stained his beard—no sluggish oozing drops
but a black rain and bloody hail poured down.

1280   So it has broken—and not on one head
but troubles mixed for husband and for wife.
The fortune of the days gone by was true
good fortune—but today groans and destruction
1285   and death and shame—of all ills can be named
not one is missing.

CHORUS: Is he now in any ease from pain?

SECOND MESSENGER: He shouts
for some one to unbar the doors and show him
to all the men of Thebes, his father's killer,
his mother's—no I cannot say the word,
it is unholy—for he'll cast himself,
1290   out of the land, he says, and not remain
to bring a curse upon his house, the curse
he called upon it in his proclamation. But
he wants for strength, aye, and some one to guide him;
his sickness is too great to bear. You, too,
1295   will be shown that. The bolts are opening.
Soon you will see a sight to waken pity
even in the horror of it.
(*Enter the blinded Oedipus.*)

CHORUS: This is a terrible sight for men to see!
I never found a worse!
1300   Poor wretch, what madness came upon you!
What evil spirit leaped upon your life
to your ill-luck—a leap beyond man's strength!
Indeed I pity you, but I cannot
look at you, though there's much I want to ask
1305   and much to learn and much to see.
I shudder at the sight of you.

OEDIPUS: O, O,
  where am I going? Where is my voice 1310
  borne on the wind to and fro?
  Spirit, how far have you sprung?

CHORUS: To a terrible place whereof men's ears
  may not hear, nor their eyes behold it.

OEDIPUS: Darkness!
  Horror of darkness enfolding, resistless, unspeakable
    visitant sped by an ill wind in haste! 1315
  madness and stabbing pain and memory
  of evil deeds I have done!

CHORUS: In such misfortunes it's no wonder
  if double weighs the burden of your grief. 1320

OEDIPUS: My friend,
  you are the only one steadfast, the only one that attends
    on me;
  you still stay nursing the blind man.
  Your care is not unnoticed. I can know 1325
  your voice, although this darkness is my world.

CHORUS: Doer of dreadful deeds, how did you dare
  so far to do despite to your own eyes?
  what spirit urged you to it?

OEDIPUS: It was Apollo, friends, Apollo,
  that brought this bitter bitterness, my sorrows to
    completion. 1330
  But the hand that struck me
  was none but my own.
  Why should I see
  whose vision showed me nothing sweet to see? 1335

CHORUS: These things are as you say.

OEDIPUS: What can I see to love?
What greeting can touch my ears with joy?
1340   Take me away, and haste—to a place out of the way!
Take me away, my friends, the greatly miserable,
1345   the most accursed, whom God too hates
above all men on earth!

CHORUS: Unhappy in your mind and your misfortune,
would I had never known you!

OEDIPUS: Curse on the man who took
1350   the cruel bonds from off my legs, as I lay in the field.
He stole me from death and saved me,
no kindly service.
Had I died then
1355   I would not be so burdensome to friends.

CHORUS: I, too, could have wished it had been so.

OEDIPUS: Then I would not have come
to kill my father and marry my mother infamously.
1360   Now I am godless and child of impurity,
begetter in the same seed that created my wretched self.
1365   If there is any ill worse than ill,
that is the lot of Oedipus.

CHORUS: I cannot say your remedy was good;
you would be better dead than blind and living.

OEDIPUS: What I have done here was best done—don't tell
1370   me
otherwise, do not give me further counsel.
I do not know with what eyes I could look
upon my father when I die and go
under the earth, nor yet my wretched mother—
those two to whom I have done things deserving
1375   worse punishment than hanging. Would the sight
of children, bred as mine are, gladden me?

No, not these eyes, never. And my city,
its towers and sacred places of the Gods,
of these I robbed my miserable self   1380
when I commanded all to drive *him* out,
the criminal since proved by God impure
and of the race of Laius.
To this guilt I bore witness against myself—
with what eyes shall I look upon my people?   1385
No. If there were a means to choke the fountain
of hearing I would not have stayed my hand
from locking up my miserable carcass,
seeing and hearing nothing; it is sweet   1390
to keep our thoughts out of the range of hurt.

Cithaeron, why did you receive me? why
having received me did you not kill me straight?
And so I had not shown to men my birth.

O Polybus and Corinth and the house,
the old house that I used to call my father's—   1395
what fairness you were nurse to, and what foulness
festered beneath! Now I am found to be
a sinner and a son of sinners. Crossroads,
and hidden glade, oak and the narrow way
at the crossroads, that drank my father's blood   1400
offered you by my hands, do you remember
still what I did as you looked on, and what
I did when I came here? O marriage, marriage!
you bred me and again when you had bred
bred children of your child and showed to men   1405
brides, wives and mothers and the foulest deeds
that can be in this world of ours.

Come—it's unfit to say what is unfit
to do.—I beg of you in God's name hide me   1410
somewhere outside your country, yes, or kill me,

or throw me into the sea, to be forever
out of your sight. Approach and deign to touch me
for all my wretchedness, and do not fear.
1415   No man but I can bear my evil doom.

CHORUS: Here Creon comes in fit time to perform
or give advice in what you ask of us.
Creon is left sole ruler in your stead.

OEDIPUS: Creon! Creon! What shall I say to him?
1420   How can I justly hope that he will trust me?
In what is past I have been proved towards him
an utter liar.
(*Enter Creon.*)

CREON: Oedipus, I've come
not so that I might laugh at you nor taunt you
with evil of the past. But if you still
are without shame before the face of men
1425   reverence at least the flame that gives all life,
our Lord the Sun, and do not show unveiled
to him pollution such that neither land
nor holy rain nor light of day can welcome.
(*To a servant.*)
1430   Be quick and take him in. It is most decent
that only kin should see and hear the troubles
of kin.

OEDIPUS: I beg you, since you've torn me
     from
my dreadful expectations and have come
in a most noble spirit to a man
that has used you vilely—do a thing for me.
I shall speak for your own good, not for my own.

1435   CREON: What do you need that you would ask of me?

OEDIPUS: Drive me from here with all the speed you can
　　to where I may not hear a human voice.

CREON: Be sure, I would have done this had not I
　　wished first of all to learn from the God the course
　　of action I should follow.

OEDIPUS:　　　　　　　　But his word   1440
　　has been quite clear to let the parricide,
　　the sinner, die.

CREON:　　　　　　　　Yes, that indeed was said.
　　But in the present need we had best discover
　　what we should do.

OEDIPUS:　　　　　　　And will you ask about
　　a man so wretched?

CREON:　　　　　　　　Now even you will trust   1445
　　the God.

OEDIPUS:　　　　　　　So. I command you—and will
　　　　beseech you—
　　to her that lies inside that house give burial
　　as you would have it; she is yours and rightly
　　you will perform the rites for her. For me—
　　never let this my father's city have me   1450
　　living a dweller in it. Leave me live
　　in the mountains where Cithaeron is, that's called
　　my mountain, which my mother and my father
　　while they were living would have made my tomb.
　　So I may die by their decree who sought
　　indeed to kill me. Yet I know this much: 1455
　　no sickness and no other thing will kill me.
　　I would not have been saved from death if not
　　for some strange evil fate. Well, let my fate
　　go where it will.
　　　　　　　　　　Creon, you need not care   1460

about my sons; they're men and so wherever
they are, they will not lack a livelihood.
But my two girls—so sad and pitiful—
whose table never stood apart from mine,
1465   and everything I touched they always shared—
O Creon, have a thought for them! And most
I wish that you might suffer me to touch them
and sorrow with them.

(Enter Antigone and Ismene, Oedipus' two daughters.)

1470   O my lord! O true noble Creon! Can I
really be touching them, as when I saw?
What shall I say?
Yes, I can hear them sobbing—my two darlings!
and Creon has had pity and has sent me
what I loved most?
1475   Am I right?

CREON: You're right: it was I gave you this
because I knew from old days how you loved them
as I see now.

OEDIPUS: God bless you for it, Creon,
and may God guard you better on your road
than he did me!
1480   O children,
where are you? Come here, come to my hands,
a brother's hands which turned your father's eyes,
those bright eyes you knew once, to what you see,
a father seeing nothing, knowing nothing,
1485   begetting you from his own source of life.
I weep for you—I cannot see your faces—
I weep when I think of the bitterness
there will be in your lives, how you must live
before the world. At what assemblages
1490   of citizens will you make one? to what

gay company will you go and not come home
in tears instead of sharing in the holiday?
And when you're ripe for marriage, who will he be,
the man who'll risk to take such infamy
as shall cling to my children, to bring hurt   1495
on them and those that marry with them? What
curse is not there? "Your father killed his father
and sowed the seed where he had sprung himself
and begot you out of the womb that held him."
These insults you will hear. Then who will marry you?   1500
No one, my children; clearly you are doomed
to waste away in barrenness unmarried.
Son of Menoeceus, since you are all the father
left these two girls, and we, their parents, both   1505
are dead to them—do not allow them wander
like beggars, poor and husbandless.
They are of your own blood.
And do not make them equal with myself
in wretchedness; for you can see them now
so young, so utterly alone, save for you only.
Touch my hand, noble Creon, and say yes.   1510
If you were older, children, and were wiser,
there's much advice I'd give you. But as it is,
let this be what you pray: give me a life
wherever there is opportunity
to live, and better life than was my father's.

CREON: Your tears have had enough of scope; now go
    within the house.   1515

OEDIPUS: I must obey, though bitter of heart.

CREON: In season, all is good.

OEDIPUS: Do you know on what conditions I obey?

CREON: You tell me them,
  and I shall know them when I hear.

OEDIPUS: That you shall send me out
  to live away from Thebes.

CREON: That gift you must ask of the God.

OEDIPUS: But I'm now hated by the Gods.

CREON: So quickly you'll obtain your
        prayer.

1520 OEDIPUS: You consent then?

CREON: What I do not mean, I do not use
        to say.

OEDIPUS: Now lead me away from here.

CREON: Let go the children, then, and
        come.

OEDIPUS: Do not take them from me.

CREON: Do not seek to be master in
        everything,
  for the things you mastered did not follow you
        throughout your life.
(*As Creon and Oedipus go out.*)

CHORUS: You that live in my ancestral Thebes, behold this
        Oedipus,—
  him who knew the famous riddles and was a man most
1525   masterful;
  not a citizen who did not look with envy on his lot—
  see him now and see the breakers of misfortune swallow
        him!
  Look upon that last day always. Count no mortal happy
        till
1530 he has passed the final limit of his life secure from pain.

OEDIPUS AT COLONUS

CHARACTERS

OEDIPUS
ANTIGONE
A STRANGER
ISMENE
THESEUS
CREON
POLYNEICES
A MESSENGER
CHORUS

OEDIPUS AT COLONUS

(Enter Oedipus, now a very old man, accompanied by his daughter Antigone.)

OEDIPUS: I am blind and old, Antigone, my child.
What country have we come to? Whose is this city?
Who will today receive the wandering
Oedipus, with the scantiest of gifts?
It's little I ask for, and still less I get,
yet it is enough for me.
My sufferings have taught me to endure—
and how long these sufferings have lasted!—
and my high breeding teaches me the same.

Child, do you see anywhere I could sit,   10
either on the common ground or in the groves
belonging to the god? Set me there securely,
that we may find out where we are; we have come to be learners
as foreigners from citizens, to do as we are told.

ANTIGONE: My poor suffering father, Oedipus!
There are towers here that protect the city; they look,
to my eyes, far off. This place is sacred—
as I would guess—it's thick with laurel,
with olives and with vines; the nightingales are singing,
thick-feathered, happily, inside the grove.   20
Here's a rough rock; bend and sit down on it.
This has been a long journey for an old man like you.

OEDIPUS: Set me now in place, watch over the blind man.

ANTIGONE: I do not need to learn that now;
time has seen to that.

OEDIPUS: Can you tell me where we are?

ANTIGONE: Athens—that much I know—but not this
place.

OEDIPUS: Yes, Athens; every traveler has told us that.

ANTIGONE: Shall I go and try to find which this place is?

30 OEDIPUS: Yes, child, if indeed there are people in it.

ANTIGONE: People there are; I think I need do nothing.
I see a man now, near us.

OEDIPUS: Are you sure? Is he really coming this way?

ANTIGONE: He is, indeed—here with us. Whatever you
have
that is suitable to say, say it; the man is here.

OEDIPUS: Sir, I have heard her say—
she has eyes for both of us—that you have come
to inquire about us. Very opportunely
you come to clear up our uncertainty.

40 STRANGER: Before you ask any more—up from this place
where you are sitting! This is no ground to tread on.

OEDIPUS: What is this place? What god is thought to
possess it?

STRANGER: It is inviolable, none may live in it. The
Goddesses
most dreadful, the daughters of Earth and Darkness,
possess it.

OEDIPUS: May I hear their sacred name to pray to them?

STRANGER: The all-seeing Eumenides, the people here call
        them,
    but they have other fair names elsewhere.
(*A silence, broken by Oedipus' words.*)

OEDIPUS: May they be gracious and receive their
        suppliant.
    For I will never go from this land—from *this* place in it!

STRANGER: What can you mean?   50

OEDIPUS: I have heard
    the watchword of my destiny.

STRANGER: No—I would certainly never have the
        boldness
    to drive you out, without the city's sanction,
    until I tell them what I am doing.

OEDIPUS: Sir, for God's sake, do not do me such
        dishonor—
    poor wanderer that I am—to deny me
    what I would beg you tell me.

STRANGER: Then speak. I *shall* not do you such dishonor.

OEDIPUS: What *is* this place on which I have set foot?   60

STRANGER: If you listen, I will tell you, whatever it is
    I know myself. All of this place is sacred;
    our holy lord Poseidon holds it. In it
    there dwells Prometheus the Titan, fire-bearing god.
    Within this land the spot you tread on
    is the Bronze Road—so it is called—
    it is the founding stone of Athens; the neighboring acres
    boast that their ruler is the Knight Colonus
    and all the people here bear his name in common.
    That is how things are, sir; here is no mere honor in
        word;   70
    the honor comes of living with the place, as theirs.

OEDIPUS: There are some, then, that live within this place?

STRANGER: Yes, surely, those that are called by the god's
    name.

OEDIPUS: Have they a sovereign, or does the word rest
    with the people?

STRANGER: They are ruled by the city's king.

OEDIPUS: And who is he
    that is so mighty both in power and word?

STRANGER: His name is Theseus, son of Aegeus, that was.

OEDIPUS: Can a messenger go from you to him?

80 STRANGER: What for?
    To tell him what, to urge his coming here?

OEDIPUS: That by small help he may reap great gains.

STRANGER: Can a blind man give such help?

OEDIPUS: There shall be sight in all the words I say.

STRANGER: Let me tell you, sir, how you will make no
    mistake;
    You are noble—anyone can see that—in all but fortune.
    Remain here where I first saw you, until I go
    and tell my fellow citizens; not those in the city,
    but citizens of *this* place. They are those to judge
90 whether you should stay here or again take the road.

OEDIPUS: Child, is the stranger gone?

ANTIGONE: Yes, he is gone;
    so, father, you may freely say everything,
    for only I am by.
(Oedipus turns towards the grove and addresses those in it.)

OEDIPUS: O solemn, dreadful-faced Ones,
    since first in this land with you I found my resting place
    and bent the knee there, be not unmindful
    of Phoebus and of me!
    For Phoebus when he prophesied those horrors,
    those many horrors for me, yet said that at the last   100
    I should find rest here, in this final country,
    when I should gain the haunt of the Dread Goddesses,
    a place of hospitality for strangers.
    There I should round my wretched life's last lap,
    a gain for those that settled me, received me,
    but a curse to those that drove me out.
    As warranty of this there should come signs,
    earthquakes and thunder, Zeus' lightning.
    Now I know well that I can trust your omen
    that guided me to this grove! Never, else, surely,   110
    had I in my traveling met with *you* first of all,
    I dry-mouthed, you that use no wine. Nor had I
    sat in this sacred undressed rock. But, Goddesses,
    as Phoebus' mouth has spoken, give my life ending
    at last, some consummation of my course,
    unless I seem to you inconsequential,
    a slave to toils, the greatest in the world.
    Come, you sweet daughters of ancient Darkness,
    come, city, called after great Pallas,
    Athens, most full of honor of any city,   120
    pity this wretched shade of the man Oedipus;
    the body that once was Oedipus is no more.

ANTIGONE: Hush! Here are some old men coming
    to spy out where we are resting.

OEDIPUS: I will be silent.
    Do you conceal me in the grove, out of the way,
    till I can find out what they will say; if we only hear,
    we can be cautious in our actions.

CHORUS OF OLD MEN, NOBLES OF ATHENS:
    Look! Who was he? And where?
130   Where has he disappeared? Where has he hurried,
    man of most impious daring? Look for him, search for
       him,
    inquire everywhere! Some wandering tramp
    he must be, not from hereabouts; else he had never
    set foot within this sacred grove
    of those violent virgins whom we tremble to name,
    whose dwelling place we pass
    with no eyes to look, and without voice to speak,
    with silent guard on lips, that no words
    may a pious mouth sound forth.

140   But now the story goes that someone has come
    who shows no reverence at all,
    and search as I may I cannot discover
    who he may be.

OEDIPUS: I am he; for I see
    by the sound of a voice, as the proverb runs.

CHORUS: Someone terrible to see,
    terrible to hear.

OEDIPUS: Do not see me as a lawbreaker—
    that I entreat you.

150 CHORUS: Zeus the Defender, who can this old man be?

OEDIPUS: Surely no one to congratulate
    on prime good fortune, guardians of this land.
    I can be clear on that; else others' eyes
    would not so guide my erring steps,
    else had my greatness not found its anchor
    on those that are but little.

CHORUS: Woe for your blinded eyes! Were you so from
      birth?
   Old and unfortunate
   is how you look to us.
   But at least if it lies with me,   160
   you should not add another curse on yourself.
   You advance too far, too far! Take heed
   lest you stumble on that grassy stretch
   where the mixing bowl
   mixes its water with the stream that runs
   sweetened with honey.
   Unlucky stranger, watch heedfully. Away!
   Step right away! He is too far away to hear!
   Do you hear, you sorrowful wanderer?
   If you want to speak and answer us,   170
   leave that forbidden place and speak
   where all may speak. Till then be silent.

OEDIPUS: Daughter, what should one think of this?

ANTIGONE: Father, we must do as other citizens here,
   yielding in what is dutiful, hearing with obedience.

OEDIPUS: Reach out your hand to me.

ANTIGONE: Here do I reach it out.

OEDIPUS: Sirs, let me not meet with injustice
   now I have trusted you and moved my ground.

CHORUS: Old man, no one shall lead you   180
   against your will, from where you rest at present.

OEDIPUS: Must I go further still?

CHORUS: Still further.

OEDIPUS: Still further?

CHORUS: Lead him, girl,
   somewhat further. *You* are listening to me.

[*R. C. Jebb, the main English commentator on Sophocles, thinks that here there are three lines lost, in interchanges between Oedipus and Antigone.*]

ANTIGONE: Follow me then, follow me
   with your blind steps; follow where I lead you.

[*Jebb thinks that a line is lost here also.*]

CHORUS: You are a stranger in a strange land,
190   poor man. Make your mind up
   to reject what this city dislikes,
   and reverence what she loves.

OEDIPUS: Lead me on, child,
   to where, my feet once more on pious footing,
   I may speak and hear.
   We must not fight against necessity.

CHORUS: Here, do not bend your steps
   beyond this block of natural stone.

OEDIPUS: Is this as you want it?

200 CHORUS: Far enough, I tell you.

OEDIPUS: May I sit?

CHORUS: Yes, sideways, on the edge of the rock,
   crouch low.

ANTIGONE: Father, let me help you—this is my task—
   step evenly with me.
   Lean your old body on my arm that loves it.
(*Oedipus groans.*)

OEDIPUS: Oh, for the mischief that haunts my mind!

CHORUS: Poor man, now that you rest,
    tell me—who are you?
    Who are you that is led so sorrowfully?   210
    May we ask what is your country?

OEDIPUS: Sirs, I have no city; please do not—

CHORUS: Do not do what, old man?

OEDIPUS: Do not ask who I am; do not push further
    in your inquiry.

CHORUS: Why so?

OEDIPUS: My breeding is full of terror.

CHORUS: Tell me.

OEDIPUS: Daughter, what am I to say?
(*He breaks into a sob.*)

CHORUS: Tell me what stock you are of, sir, and your
        father.   220

OEDIPUS: (*sobbing*) What will become of me, child?

ANTIGONE: Tell them. You are as far as you can go.

OEDIPUS: I will tell them, then. Indeed, I cannot hide it.

CHORUS: You are slow and hesitant. Be quick and tell us.

OEDIPUS: Do you know a son
    of Laius?

CHORUS: Oh, yes, yes!

OEDIPUS: He was of the family of the Labdacids.

CHORUS: O Zeus!

OEDIPUS: The miserable Oedipus.   230

CHORUS: And you are *he*?

OEDIPUS: Do not be so terrified
at what I say.

CHORUS: (*cries out*)

OEDIPUS: A doomed man.

CHORUS: (*cries out*)

OEDIPUS: Daughter,
what will become of me *now*?

CHORUS: Out of this place, out of it!

240 OEDIPUS: And your promise? What will that be?

CHORUS: Punishment is not the due lot of anyone
who but requites what is already done to him.
Trickery matching others' trickery gives
pain and not pleasure in return.
Up from this place!—and from this country where
you have found an anchorage!
Do not fix upon my city
some further debt to bear.

ANTIGONE: Sirs, you have honor in your hearts,
250 but you cannot bear with my father, old and blind,
because you have heard the tale
of acts done in unconsciousness!
Yet, sirs, take pity on my wretched self;
I who beg you for my father only.
I beg you, with eyes not blinded, facing your eyes,
as though I came of your own blood,
that he, in his unhappiness, win your mercy.
What happens to us lies in your hands,
as though you were a god.
260 Come, grant me a favor—though I scarce look for it—
I entreat you by all that is dear to you—

by child or wife, by duty or by god.
No matter where you look, you will find no man
who can escape if a god leads him on.

CHORUS: Why, know, you child of Oedipus, that you and
      he
both win our pity for your calamity.
But we dread judgment from the gods. We cannot
say more than what we have said to you already.

OEDIPUS: What is the good of a glorious reputation
if it is like an idly flowing stream?   270
They say that Athens is the holiest of cities,
say that she always rescues the injured stranger,
that she alone is able to defend him.
Where are these things for me? You moved me out
from the safety of this rock; then drive me out
forth from your country—fearing my name alone!
Surely not what I am nor what I have done.
Indeed, what I have done
is suffering rather than doing, if I were to tell you
the story of both my parents, which makes you dread
      me.   280
That I know well. How can my nature be evil,
when all I did was matching others' actions?
Even had I done what I did full consciously,
even so, I would not have been evil.
But the truth is, I knew nothing
when I came where I did. Yet *they* knew—
those by whom I suffered—knew what they did.
It was meant to be my death.
Therefore, sirs, I beseech you by the gods,
since you took me from my place of safety, save me now. 290
Do not, as honoring the gods, fail to give those gods
their dues of recognition. Think that they look
upon those that respect the gods and those

who do not so—among all men in the world.
Never yet has the wicked man got clear away,
escaping them. Take the side of those gods, do not dim
    the glory
of Athens by serving deeds of wickedness.
Rescue me, guard me; do not see the ugliness
of my face to its dishonor.

300   I am here as sacred and pious both,
and bringing benefit to your citizens.
When your lord comes here—whoever is your leader—
you shall hear all and understand it all.
In the time between these words and his arrival
do not turn villains.

CHORUS: We needs must fear, old man, those haunted
    thoughts
coming from you; the words that clothe them are not
    light.
It is enough for me that this land's princes
shall know the matter through and through.

310   OEDIPUS: Sirs, where is the ruler of this land?

CHORUS: He is in his father's city, in our country.
The man who sent me here has gone to fetch him.

OEDIPUS: Do you believe that he will care so much
to give a thought to a blind man—that he will come
himself to see me?

CHORUS: He surely will when he has heard your name.

OEDIPUS: Who is there that will bring *that* word to him?

CHORUS: It is a long road here; there are many travelers
and many tales of theirs; these he will hear

320   and come; do not trouble for that. Your name, old man,
has pierced the ears of many; were he asleep

or slow to move, yet when he hears
of *you,* he will come quickly to this place.

OEDIPUS: Well, may he come, with good luck for this city,
and for me, too! For what good man is there
who is no friend to himself?

ANTIGONE: Zeus, what shall I say? What am I to think,
father?

OEDIPUS: What is it, Antigone, my child?

ANTIGONE: I see a girl
coming towards us riding an Etnean horse;   330
on her head is a Thessalian bonnet
which shields her from the sun. What do I say?
Is it really she? or not? does my mind cheat me?
It is—it isn't—I cannot tell—
It *is* she and no other. Her eyes are all aglow
as she comes to welcome me. That shows it is she—
she and no other, Ismene, my darling!

OEDIPUS: What is it you say, child?

ANTIGONE: That I see your daughter,
my own sister. Soon you will know,   340
hearing her voice.

ISMENE: Dear father and sister—how sweet are both those
names!
How hard it was to find you, and now you are found,
how hard, again, to see you, for my tears!

OEDIPUS: You have really come, my child?

ISMENE: Father—how hard to see you so!

OEDIPUS: You are really there, child!

ISMENE: Yes, though it was hard to come here.

OEDIPUS: Touch me, my child.

350   ISMENE: I touch you both alike.

OEDIPUS: Sisters. True sisters both!

ISMENE: How wretched this life of ours.

OEDIPUS: You mean, her life and mine?

ISMENE: Yes, and mine too.

OEDIPUS: Why have you come?

ISMENE: Through care of you.

OEDIPUS: Because you longed to see me?

ISMENE: Yes, and to tell you things
          with my own tongue. My companion here
360   was the only trusty servant that I have.

OEDIPUS: Where are those brothers of your blood
          to do us service now?

ISMENE: They are where they are.
          This is a terrible time for them.

OEDIPUS: Those two are like in everything
          to the ways of Egypt,
          both in their nature and in how they live.
          For in that country the men sit within doors
          working at the loom, while the wives go out
370   to get the daily bread.
          So, children, those two brothers of yours, who should
          bear the stress and strain, keep house within, like girls,
          and you, in their stead, struggle to bear my troubles.
          You, Antigone, since you ceased to be a child,
          and had grown strong enough, wandered with me
            always,
          to your unhappiness, guiding an old man's steps.

Many a time you strayed in the wild woods,
without a bite to eat and barefoot;
many a wet day, many a burning sunlight
you toiled through; you never thought   380
of home or comfort in comparison
with the need to earn your father the means to live.
And you, Ismene, in the old time came to me
unknown to the Cadmeans, with all their oracles
that spoke about this carcass of mine.
You were my trusty guard when I was hunted
out of Theban land.
But now again what tale have you to tell me,
your father? What mission started you from your home?
I am very sure you are not empty-handed,   390
but carry with you some terror affecting me.

ISMENE: What I endured in looking for you, father—
in trying to find where you were living—
let me leave alone. I do not want to suffer
twice over, in the doing and telling both.
But I have come here to declare to you
the evils that befell your unhappy sons.

At first their passionate wish—as it was Creon's—
was to leave the throne to him, and not pollute
the city further. They looked sensibly   400
at the old destruction that lay on their breeding,
which indeed beset your unlucky house.
But now stirred by some god
and by some sinfulness of mind themselves,
a deadly spirit of competition
has entered these thrice unhappy beings
to grasp the government and the monarchy;
and the younger born, his hot blood up,
would rob his elder brother Polyneices
of the throne and has banished him the country.   410

The elder, as rumor multiplied declares,
went into exile in hollow Argos,
and there took to himself a new marriage tie
and for new friends new fellow spearmen,
his aim that Argos should possess in honor
the land of Thebes or else exalt to heaven
the Theban power by the defeat of Argos.
This is no empty sum of words, my father;
they are deeds and terrible. At what point the gods
420   will pity your tribulations I cannot guess.

OEDIPUS: Did you really hope the gods would take any
    heed
of me, enough some day to rescue me?

ISMENE: I do, my father, from these present oracles.

OEDIPUS: And what are they? What has been prophesied,
my child?

ISMENE: That you shall one day be desired
by Thebes, yes, living and dead you *shall* be,
for their own welfare's sake.

OEDIPUS: How can anyone's welfare depend
430   on such as I am?

ISMENE: With you, they say, there rests
their victory.

OEDIPUS: When I *am* no longer
then am I a man?

ISMENE: Yes, father, for today the gods exalt you;
then they destroyed you.

OEDIPUS: It is a poor thing to exalt the old
when he fell in his youth.

ISMENE: Still, you must know that Creon
　　for these very causes is coming here,　　　　　440
　　and shortly, without loss of time.

OEDIPUS: What would he do,
　　my daughter? Explain that to me.

ISMENE: They want to place you near the land of Thebes,
　　to own you, still not letting your foot tread
　　within the borders of their country.

OEDIPUS: What good can I do, lying outside their doors?

ISMENE: The place you lie in—if it suffer wrong—
　　will be a heavy curse on them.

OEDIPUS: One needs no god to have the knowledge of
　　that.　　　　　450

ISMENE: Well, that is why they want to have you as an ally,
　　near to their land, but not as your own master.

OEDIPUS: Will they let the shadowing dust of Thebes lie
　　on me?

ISMENE: No, for the guilt of family bloodletting
　　debars it, father.

OEDIPUS: Then they will never own me.

ISMENE: So shall there be a heavy weight of sorrow
　　upon the Thebans.

OEDIPUS: In what conjunction, child, shall this come to
　　pass?

ISMENE: When your anger strikes them, as they stand on
　　your grave.　　　　　460

OEDIPUS: What you say now—from whom did you hear
    that?

ISMENE: The sacred envoys when they came back from
    Delphi.

OEDIPUS: And that was, truly, what Phoebus said about
    me?

ISMENE: So the men said that came to Thebes from
    Delphi.

OEDIPUS: Did either of my sons know this about me?

ISMENE: Both of them equally; both knew it well.

OEDIPUS: And then those villains, when they heard of it,
    longed for me less than for this throne of theirs?

ISMENE: I hate to hear that said, but I must bear it.

OEDIPUS: Then may the gods never quench their fated
470   quarrel
    and may it lie in *my* hands to determine
    the end of the fight, which now they seek so eagerly
    with their raised spears. If that shall happen
    neither he that presently holds throne and scepter
    shall remain where he is; nor he the exile
    shall return home. I am their father
    and when I was dishonored and driven out
    from my own land, they never hindered it,
    nor helped defend me; as far as they could do it,
    it was those two expelled me; by them I was proclaimed
480   exile.
    You might say that *then* I also willed it so,
    and that the city granted me that gift.
    This is not so; for on the day itself
    when my spirit seethed, and death was dearest to me,
    yes, death by stoning, no one would help me to it.

But when time had gone by,
and all the agony had mellowed,
when I felt my agony had outrun itself
in punishing my former sins—it was then and then
the city drove me out—after all that time!—   490
in my despite—and these, these sons of mine,
could have helped me, their father, but they would not.
No, for the lack of one short word from them
I was banished, a beggar, to wander forever.
But it was from *these,* girls as they are,
as far as their nature could, I had my sustenance,
and ground to tread on without fear,
and the support of kinfolk.
Those other two, above their father's claims
chose sovereignty, wielding the scepter,   500
and their land's lordship. No, they will never win me
to be their ally, nor shall there ever come
profit to them from their reign in Thebes:
that I know well, both from Ismene's oracles,
which I now hear, and when I recollect
those of old days which Phoebus has accomplished
now in this time.
So let them send Creon to fetch me in,
or anyone else of power within their city,
for if you, my foreign friends, are willing,   510
backed by those solemn goddesses
that are your champions, to grant me your protection,
you will win for your city
a mighty service and for enemies, trouble.

CHORUS: Oedipus, you certainly deserve pity,
    yourself and your daughters; and since you add to the
        count
    that you will be the savior of our country,
    may I suggest to you thoughts perhaps useful?

OEDIPUS: Dear friend: do but be my champion,
520   and be assured I will do all you tell me.

CHORUS: Make an atonement to those deities
   you came to first, when you trespassed on their ground.

OEDIPUS: In what fashion shall I do it? Tell me, sirs.

CHORUS: First bring a sacred draught from the everlasting
   springs there; and let the hands that bring it be pure.

OEDIPUS: And when I take this draught unsullied—what
   then?

CHORUS: There are bowls there, work of a skillful maker;
   crown the top of each, and the handles at either side.

OEDIPUS: With twigs or flocks of wool—or how shall I do
   it?

CHORUS: With a flock of wool, new shorn, from a ewe
530   lamb.

OEDIPUS: Very well; after that what must I do?

CHORUS: Pour your offerings, with your face towards the
   first dawn.

OEDIPUS: Shall I pour them from the vessels that you
   speak of?

CHORUS: Yes, in three streams; the last must empty the
   bowl.

OEDIPUS: What shall I fill the third with before I set it?
   Tell me that, too.

CHORUS: With water and with honey.
   Do not bring wine near it.

OEDIPUS: And when the dark-shading earth has drunk
   of it?

CHORUS: Then with both hands, taking nine sprigs of
    olive,   540
  lay them on it; and say this prayer over them.

OEDIPUS: *That* I would hear—that is the greatest thing!

CHORUS: "As we call these the Kindly Ones, with kindly
  hearts may they welcome this suppliant for his saving."
  So pray, or those who speak for you.
  But say the words inaudibly; do not raise your voice.
  Then go away—and do not look behind you.
  If you do this, I will stand by your side and welcome.
  Otherwise, sir, I will fear on your behalf.

OEDIPUS: My children, you have heard the strangers who
    live here?   550

ANTIGONE: We have heard; do you but tell us what to do.

OEDIPUS: I cannot go myself; I fail in strength
  and sight, my double weakness.
  One of you must go and do this thing,
  for I think that one soul—be it but a well-wisher's—
  can pay the debt for tens of thousands.
  Quickly now; but do not leave me alone.
  My body cannot move, lonely of help,
  nor without guidance.

ISMENE: I will go to do it.   560
  But I must know where I should find the place.

CHORUS: On the other side of the grove, girl. If you need
    anything,
  a man lives there who will tell you.

ISMENE: I will go to my task; Antigone,
  stay here and guard our father; for a parent's sake,
  whatever trouble there is—if there is any—
  does not count.

CHORUS: It is a dreadful thing, sir,
    to awaken again an old ill that lies quiet.
570   Yet still I long to know—

OEDIPUS: What? What do you mean?

CHORUS: Of the pain that besets your life,
    so remediless, so wretched—

OEDIPUS: Do not, I beg you—
    I am your guest; you were kind to me.
    Do not lay bare my sufferings;
    they are beyond shame.

CHORUS: It is a story that has spread far;
    it doesn't die out. I would like to hear the right of it.

580 OEDIPUS: (*moans*)

CHORUS: Endure the pain, I say.

OEDIPUS: Oh, oh.

CHORUS: Do as I beg you. I gave you what *you* asked.

OEDIPUS: I bore the worst of sufferings—but for deeds—
    be God my witness!—done without knowledge.
    In all this there was nothing of conscious choice.

CHORUS: How was it?

OEDIPUS: It was the city bound me,
    in utter ignorance, in a deadly marriage,
590   in fated ruin, that came with my wife.

CHORUS: Was it then, as I hear,
    that you filled your bed
    with your mother to your infamy?

OEDIPUS: Oh, it is death to hear it said,
    strangers. These two girls of mine—

CHORUS: You mean—

OEDIPUS: Yes, my children, they are the two
curses upon me.

CHORUS: Zeus!

OEDIPUS: They sprang from the womb that bore me also.   600

CHORUS: Then they are your children and—

OEDIPUS: Their father's sisters, too.

[*The passage that follows is difficult to understand. The Chorus
has from the first, on hearing Oedipus' name, seemed to know the
story. Apparently this may not be the case—at least the story in its
entirety. There is another version of the myth, a fragment of
Theban epic known to Pausanias, the very much later author of the
geography of Greece, according to which the children of Oedipus
here, Ismene and Antigone, are the children of his second wife,
Euryganeia. Odyssey XI 271 is not explicit on this, but there are
other aspects of its difference from our version—e.g., after Jocasta
killed herself, Oedipus went on ruling Thebes. R. C. Jebb thinks it
was the Attic dramatists who first introduced into the story the
bearing of the incest on the daughters (Jebb, commentary on O. C.
534). If this is right, the Chorus in the passage following this
does make a genuinely new discovery from Oedipus. They may have
been following till then the other and older version of the myth. The
half lines of each speaker, each completing the statement, is far
from anything we find dramatic. The whole is written in semi-
lyrical meters and was probably delivered in a semi-ritualized
manner, a kind of singsong interchange, almost like a dirge. It is of
course extremely difficult for a translator to render tolerably.*]

CHORUS: Oh, oh!

OEDIPUS: Ten thousand horrors sweep back upon me.

CHORUS: You have suffered—

OEDIPUS: What I can never forget.

CHORUS: But you *did*—

OEDIPUS: I *did* nothing.

CHORUS: How can that be?

610 OEDIPUS: I received a gift
     for serving the city—would to God I had never won
          it!—
     for my heart is broken.

CHORUS: Unhappy man! But you did a murder.

OEDIPUS: How a murder? What is it you would know?

CHORUS: Your father's murder.

OEDIPUS: You strike me again, wound upon wound.

CHORUS: But you killed him.

OEDIPUS: Yes, I killed him, but he had from me—

CHORUS: What?

620 OEDIPUS: Something of justice.

CHORUS: How can that be?

OEDIPUS: I will tell you.
     Those that I killed would have killed me.
     So in law I am innocent and came to all this
     in ignorance.

CHORUS: Here is our king, Theseus, son of Aegeus,
     to do what the news of you summoned him to do.

THESEUS: In time past, son of Laius, I have heard from
          many
     of the bloody blinding of your eyes—and I recognized
          you.
630 Now as I heard more on my journey here
     I am in greater certainty.

The clothes you wear and your unhappy face
show us clearly who you are. Because you have
my pity, unfortunate Oedipus, I would ask you
what is this supplication you urge on Athens
and on myself—you and the poor girl beside you?
Tell me. You must tell me something dreadful indeed
to make me turn away from you.
For my part I know what it means,
myself, to be brought up in exile,   640
as you are in exile. I too in a foreign country
wrestled with dangers to my life, more than anyone else.
So there is surely no stranger, such as you,
from whom I would turn my face, nor help to save.
For I am very certain I am but a man:
as such, I have of tomorrow no greater share
than you have.

OEDIPUS: Theseus, your nobleness in one short speech
    has left me the necessity of saying little.
    You have said about me all that is true—   650
    who I am, from what father born, from what country
        come.
    All that is left me to say is what I want,
    and then the story is told.

THESEUS: Tell me; let me know.

OEDIPUS: I come to give you this wretched carcass of
        mine,
    a gift to you; to look at, no great matter,
    but no beautiful body will give you such gains as it will.

THESEUS: What is this gain you claim to bring with you?

OEDIPUS: In time you will know—but the time is not yet,
    I think.

THESEUS: When will your benefit be shown?   660

OEDIPUS: When I die and you shall have been my burial
man.

THESEUS: You ask about the last moments of your life;
what lies between this and then
you either forget or have no heed of.

OEDIPUS: Yes:
when that is given, my whole harvest is in.

THESEUS: The favor you ask me lies in small compass,
then?

OEDIPUS: Watch that; it is no easy fight to win.

THESEUS: Do you mean between your sons and me?

670 OEDIPUS: Yes.
They wish to carry me away to Thebes.

THESEUS: Well, if you are willing—
exile is not a fine thing.

OEDIPUS: When I myself was willing they would not let
me.

THESEUS: You are being foolish; anger does not sit well
with folk in trouble.

OEDIPUS: Rebuke me when you understand, and not till
then.

THESEUS: Then tell me. True, without knowledge I should
not speak.

OEDIPUS: I have suffered, Theseus, terribly, evils upon
evils.

680 THESEUS: You mean what befell your family from of old?

OEDIPUS: No. That is the talk of everyone in Greece.

THESEUS: What then is your suffering beyond all men's
    endurance?

OEDIPUS: This is how it is. I was banished from my own
    country
  by my own sons, return forever denied me,
  because I killed my father.

THESEUS: How then would they send for you
  if it is but to settle you apart?

OEDIPUS: It is the mouth of God will force them to it.

THESEUS: What is it, then, they fear foretold in oracles?

OEDIPUS: That they must be smitten by this land of yours.　690

THESEUS: But how should there be bitterness between
  them and myself?

OEDIPUS: O dearest son of Aegeus:
  only the gods know neither age nor death;
  everything else all-mastering time confounds.
  The strength of earth, the strength of body, dies;
  trust dies, distrust comes into blossoming.
  The same breath does not blow from man to man,
  constant in friendship, nor in city towards city.
  It may be now, it may be later, sometime　　　　700
  the sweet turns bitter, and then again to friendship.
  If now the day is bright betwixt you and Thebes,
  uncounted time in course will breed uncounted
  nights and days, shattering with the spear
  those right hands presently clasped in harmony.
  The cause will be so slight!
  At that time my body hidden in earth and sleeping
  will coldly drink their hot blood,
  if Zeus be still Zeus and if Zeus' son
  Phoebus speak clearly.　　　　　　　　　　710

But it is not pleasant
to speak the words that should lie undisturbed.
Let me stop where I began; do you only keep
the pledge you gave me and you will never say
that you received as dweller in this land,
a worthless fellow, Oedipus—
unless the gods shall cheat me.

CHORUS: My lord, this man has talked like this before,
as though he would do something for our country.

720   THESEUS: Who would reject goodwill in such a man?
In the first place, forever a hearth between us
speaks of guest-friendship and a spear alliance.
And then he has come a suppliant of these Goddesses,
and promises to this land and myself
no inconsiderable recompense.
These matters claim my reverence and so
I will not reject his claim upon my gratitude.
I will make him our citizen. If it be his pleasure,
this stranger's, to remain here I will charge you
730   to guard him. (*Turning to Oedipus.*)
                        Or, if you please to come with me,
Oedipus, I submit to your judgment.
It shall be as you choose.

OEDIPUS: May God send blessings on such men as you!

THESEUS: What would you, then? Will you come to my
    home?

OEDIPUS: I would—if it were lawful. But this place here—

THESEUS: What would you do in "this place"? I will not
    oppose you.

OEDIPUS: It is *here* I will conquer those that cast me out.

THESEUS: This would be a great gift of your staying here.

OEDIPUS: If you stand fast by what you said and do it. 740

THESEUS: You need not fear for me. I will not fail you.

OEDIPUS: I will not put you on your oath like someone
base.

THESEUS: No oath will give you more than my bare word.

OEDIPUS: What will you do then—

THESEUS: What is it you fear most?

OEDIPUS: Some will come here—

THESEUS: My friends will take care of *that*.

OEDIPUS: See you do not fail me—

THESEUS: Do not tell me my duty.

OEDIPUS: It is inevitable that I should fear. 750

THESEUS: *I* do not fear.

OEDIPUS: You do not know the threats—

THESEUS: I do know that no one
will take you out of here against my will.
There are many threats, and many threatening words
issue out of anger. When the mind is master of itself,
the threats have vanished.
Perhaps these people had strength enough to speak
dreadful things of your carrying off, but *I* know
the sea to sail between us will seem long, 760
poor prospects for a voyage. I would say to you
"Be of good cheer" even without my judgment,
since Phoebus sent you hither. Even though *I* were not
here,
my *name* will guard you against ill-usage.

CHORUS: Here are the fairest homesteads of the world,
here in this country, famed for its horses,
 stranger,
where you have come:
Here to Colonus, gleaming white,
where the nightingale in constant trilling song
770   cries from beneath the green leaves,
where she lives in the wine dark ivy
and the dark foliage of ten thousand berries,
safe from the sun, safe from the wind
of every storm, god's place, inviolable.
Where Dionysus the reveler paces
thronged by the nymphs his nurses.

Here there blooms, fed by heaven's dew,
daily and ever, the lovely-clustered narcissus,
the ancient crown of the Great Goddesses,
780   and also the golden gleaming crocus.
Nor fail the wandering springs
that feed the streams of Cephisus,
but daily and ever the river
with his pure waters gives increase
over the swelling bosom of the land.
This country the bands of the Muses
have not disdained
nor yet Aphrodite of the Golden Reins.
There is a thing too, of which no other like
790   I have heard in Asian land,
nor as ever grown in the great Dorian
island of Pelops,
a plant unconquered and self-renewing,
a terror that strikes the spear-armed enemy,
a plant that flourishes greatest here,
leaf of gray olive,
nourishing our children.
It shall not be rendered impotent

by the young nor by him that lives with old age,
destroying it with violence,   800
for the ever-living eye of Morian Zeus
looks upon it—and gray-eyed Athene also.

Yet another matter of praise have I
for this my mother city,
gift of a great god, our land's great boast,
that it is horse master, colt breaker, master of the
    sea.
Son of Cronus, Lord Poseidon,
you it is who have set her in that glory.
For you are the one who in these roads first
established the bit to control the horse,   810
and the oar, too, well fitted to the hand
leaps marvelously in the sea,
following the hundred-footed Nereids.

ANTIGONE: Land with praises richly celebrated,
now be it yours to make those praises shine.

OEDIPUS: What is there new, child?

ANTIGONE: Creon draws near.
Here he is—and with followers.

OEDIPUS: (*to the Chorus*) Old men,
my friends, now manifest, I beg you,   820
the last goal of my safety.

CHORUS: Courage!
That safety shall be yours. If *I* am old,
the strength of Attica has not grown old.

CREON: Sirs, noble gentlemen of this land,
I see your eyes have suddenly taken fright
at my intrusion. I beg you, do not fear
nor speak ill words to me.
I have come with no determination

830 to offer any violence. I am old myself
and know I have come to a city powerful
as any is in Greece.
I was sent, old as I am, to urge this man
to come with me to Thebes.
No single person sent me. I have my orders
from the whole commonality. They sent *me*
because it was I who was most concerned
(because of our relationship) to sorrow,
most of all within our city, for *his* troubles.

840 Unhappy Oedipus, hear me and come home!
All the Cadmean people summon you, and rightly,
and most of all do I, in the proportion
that I must be the worst of scoundrels
if I felt no pain at these your sufferings.
I see you an unfortunate wretch, a foreigner,
a beggar always and your sightless journeyings
propped on this one girl only. I could not believe
that she could fall to such a depth of misery
as this unhappy child here, tending you

850 and your life in daily beggary, young as she is,
but with no part in marriage, a ready victim
to be seized and raped by anyone.
It *is* a miserable reproach, is it not?,
that I have cast on you—and on me and all our breed.
There is no hiding it. It's plain.
But, Oedipus, it is you—I beg you—by our fathers'
  gods, *you*,
listen to my words! it is *you* should hide it,
by willingness to come to your own city
and to the house that was your fathers'.

860 Greet this city kindly—of course she has deserved it!—
but your own country should be honored more,
in justice, for she bred you up at first.

OEDIPUS: You would dare anything; from every plea of
     justice
  you can extract some means of trickery.
  Why do you try so? Why do you want
  to catch me once again, when the catching will hurt
     most?
  In the old time I was so sick in my troubles
  that it had been my pleasure to be exiled;
  but then when I was willing, you were not
  to give me any such favor. But when my anger   870
  was sated of itself, when living in that house
  had become sweet to me, you threw me out,
  you banished me. In that day this kinship you speak of
  was no way dear to you.
  And now again, when you see this city friendly
  to my staying, when you see all the people friendly,
  you try to tear me out, the harshness of your message
  so softly rendered!
  Yet, what pleasure can you have in showing kindness
  to those that will not welcome it? It is as if   880
  one begged for something, but was given nothing,
  nor was there wish to help; but when the spirit
  was sated with what one had sought for, then only,
  one got the gift, when the grace carried no grace.
  Surely this is an empty pleasure you gain.
  And that indeed is what you have given me,
  where the words are good and the substance evil.
  I will show these people what a villain you are.
  You have come to bring me, yes, but *not* to bring me
     home
  but to set me in a dwelling apart—but near you,   890
  so there will be no trouble with Athens for your city.
  You will not succeed, no, instead
  my spirit shall dwell forever, a curse,
  a curse upon your country.

For these sons of mine, this is my prayer—
so much of their father's earth as to make their graves.
Am I not wiser than you in Theban matters?
Far wiser, for I learn from clearer speakers,
Phoebus and Zeus himself, that is his father.
900   But you have come here, a mouth suborned,
but with a right sharp tongue. For all that, in your
         speaking
you will win more harm than safety.
However, I know I am not persuading you.
Get gone!
Let us live here; even as it is
we would live well enough
if we are content.

CREON: Who do you think has had the worst of it
in this discussion? I in respect to you
910   or you towards yourself?

OEDIPUS: What I find most pleasant is your failure
to persuade me or these men here.

CREON: You miserable creature, clearly you haven't
been able to grow wise, with all your years.

OEDIPUS: You have a clever tongue, but I never knew a
         just man
speak equally well on every plea.

CREON: Saying much is one thing, seasonableness another.

OEDIPUS: As though *your* words were few but very
         seasonable!

CREON: Not seasonable, of course, for one so clever
920   as you are.

OEDIPUS: Away with you! I will speak on these men's
         behalf:
do not watch and hem me in; this is where I live.

CREON: I call these men to witness, not you, for what you
have answered
to those of us who are your family. If ever I catch you—

OEDIPUS: How will you catch me in despite of these allies?

CREON: I can hurt you enough without such action.

OEDIPUS: What lies behind these threats of yours?

CREON: You have
two daughters, one of whom I have seized
and sent away. The other I will take soon.   930

OEDIPUS: O God!

CREON: Soon you will have more reason to cry out.

OEDIPUS: You have my child?

CREON: And will have *this* one soon.

OEDIPUS: Sirs, what will you do? Will you betray your
trust?
Will you not get rid of this unholy wretch?

CHORUS: Here, you, sir, off with you! What you are doing
is utterly unjust. So is what you *have* done.

CREON: (*to his servants*) It is high time for you to lead her
off.
If she won't go willingly, force her!   940

ANTIGONE: What refuge have I? What help can I find
from god or man?

CHORUS: What are you about, sir?

CREON: I will not take the man, but *she* is mine.

OEDIPUS: O, princes of this country!

CHORUS: Sir, this is injustice!

CREON: No, it is just.

CHORUS: How can it be just?

CREON: I take my own.

950 OEDIPUS: O city of Athens!

CHORUS: What are you doing, sir? Release her at once.
If not—a trial of strength between us!

CREON: Give way!

CHORUS: Not to you while this is your purpose.

CREON: You will fight with Thebes, if you do me an
injury.

OEDIPUS: Did I not say
this is how it would be?

CHORUS: Release that girl at once.

CREON: Do not give orders
960 that you cannot enforce.

CHORUS: I tell you take your hands off her!

CREON: I tell you
take a walk!

CHORUS: Come, countrymen of ours, come here, come
here!
The city is made nothing of, our city,
by this violence. Come here, come here to us!

ANTIGONE: Friends, I am dragged away.

OEDIPUS: Where are you, child?

ANTIGONE: They are forcing me away!

970 OEDIPUS: Reach me your hands!

ANTIGONE: I cannot, I cannot.

CREON: (*to the servants*) Bring her away, you!

OEDIPUS: O God, O God!

CREON: Well, on these crutches you will not travel again.
But since you are determined to beat your country,
and your family at whose command I do
what I do—although I am their sovereign lord as well—
enjoy your victory. In time you will know,
I am certain, that what you do to yourself at present
is nothing good, nor what you did before,   980
when in the teeth of your friends you yielded to temper.
It is your temper which constantly ruins you.

CHORUS: Stop right there, sir.

CREON: I warn you, do not touch me.

CHORUS: Give back the girls. Else you will not go from
here.

CREON: You will soon give my city a greater prize
for our security. I will take more than these.

CHORUS: What will you do next?

CREON: I will take and carry *him* off.

CHORUS: An outrageous threat!   990

CREON: It shall be executed.

CHORUS: Unless this country's ruler thwarts you.

OEDIPUS: A shameless thing to say! Will you seize me
indeed?

CREON: Hold your tongue!

OEDIPUS: May the gods of this place
not take away my tongue from uttering this curse!
You villain: after the violence to my onetime eyes,
you have wrenched from me the one poor eye I had left.
May the Sun-God that sees all give you and your seed
an old age like this of mine!

CREON: Do you see that, you people of this country?

OEDIPUS: They see both you and me; they understand
I am wronged in deeds, my defense, words only.

CREON: I'll not hold back my anger. I will bring him away by force,
although I am alone and slow with age.

OEDIPUS: (*cries out*)

CHORUS: You have a bold spirit, sir, to think to come here,
and do as you do.

CREON: Yes, I believe I have.

CHORUS: If you are right, I will no longer think
Athens a city.

CREON: With a just cause the weak subdue the strong.

OEDIPUS: Do you hear what he says?

CHORUS: But he will not act it—
Zeus knows!

CREON: Zeus maybe knows—not you.

CHORUS: The insolence of this!

CREON: Insolence you must put up with.

CHORUS: You people, and the rulers of this state, come
       here to us!
   Come quickly. These men will cross the border.   1020
(*Theseus enters.*)

THESEUS: What is this noise about? What has happened
       here?
   You have stopped me in my sacrifice to the sea-god,
   lord of Colonus here: I was at the altar.
   What fear made you do that? Tell me. I want
   to know it all, why I have been made to hasten
   faster than I liked to this place here.

OEDIPUS: Dearest of men, I recognize your voice. I have
       suffered
   dreadfully, right now, at this man's hands.

THESEUS: What happened? Who has injured you? Speak!

OEDIPUS: Creon here, before your eyes, has taken my   1030
   two children, all that I had.

THESEUS: What is this you say?

OEDIPUS: You have heard what he did to me.

THESEUS: (*points to his servants*) Here, quickly, one of
       you go to the altars,
   urge all the people to leave the sacrifice
   and hurry, on horseback and on foot,
   at a full gallop to that place hereabouts
   where the two traveled roads combine,
   so that the girls won't get across and I,
   worsted by violence, become a mockery   1040
   to my guest-friend.
   Away you go! Quickly! As I told you.
   For you, Creon, if I went as far in anger
   as you deserve, you would not go without

marks of my hands upon you.
However, such laws as he imported here
shall be made to fit him—these and no others.
(*He speaks directly to Creon.*)

You shall not leave this country until you bring here
these girls for me to see. What you have done
1050   is a disgrace to me, and your own blood,
and to your country. You came within this city
that makes a practice of justice and determines
nothing without a law. You then throw aside
her lawful institutions by your invasion.
You take what you want, making them yours by force.
Apparently you thought this city quite unmanned
or some slave place, and me a nobody.
Yet it is not Thebes has taught you to be so bad.
They do not usually rear men as wrongdoers,
1060   nor would the Thebans praise you if they heard
you had violated what are mine and the gods'
    possessions,
dragging out the helpless creatures that are their
    suppliants.
I certainly never would have put foot on your soil—
not if I had the justest cause in the world—
without permission of the governors, whoever.
I would not have harried and plundered; I would have
    known
how I ought—a foreigner among citizens—
to conduct myself. But you dishonor
a city that has not merited dishonor—
1070   your own city; and your years, so many,
show you an old man still empty of wisdom.
So I tell you now what I have said before;
let someone bring those girls here—quickly, too—
unless you want to be a resident alien

of Athens, under constraint, not voluntary.
That is what I have to say. It comes from my full
   meaning,
not simply from my tongue.

CHORUS: You see what you have come to, sir. You appear
   to be of those who are just, but what you do
   is found to be evil.   1080

CREON: Of course I did not think this city unmanned,
   son of Aegeus, nor yet without wisdom as you claim,
   when I did this thing I did. I thought
   that no one would ever feel such eager love
   for those that are my kinfolk that they would keep them
   against my wishes! I knew you would not accept
   a man who is his father's killer, unholy,
   nor one whose marriage is found accursed,
   a union of mother and son.
   I knew the Areopagus, that grave council   1090
   which belongs to this country, would not permit
   such outcasts as these to live within its realm.
   It was because I was confident of this
   that I laid my hands upon this quarry.
   Even then I would not have done so had he not cursed
      me
   myself with bitter curses, and my breed.
   This is what he did to me, and I determined
   to give as good again. Anger knows no old age,
   except in death. No sting touches the dead.
   That is the case; do as you will about it.   1100
   However just my cause, I am all alone;
   that makes me weak; but yet as you shall act,
   old as I am, I will try to act against you.

OEDIPUS: Spirit lost to shame, whom does the insult
          light on,
      on you or me since both of us are old?
      Your mouth is wide with taunts against me—murders,
      and incest and calamity, which I bore,
      poor wretch, involuntarily: the gods' pleasure!
      Perhaps they were angry against my people of old.
1110 You cannot find in me, taken by myself,
      an offense to reproach me with of such a greatness
      to occasion such dreadful sins as I committed
      against me and mine.

      Tell me this:
      if some god-utterance came to my father
      given by oracles, that he should die by the hand
      of his son, how can you justly taunt me with that,
      who then owned neither father's seed nor mother's
          womb,
      but was a creature still unborn?
1120 If then I appeared, as I did to my sorrow,
      and came to blows with my father and murdered him,
      knowing nothing of what I did, nor who he was,
      how can you be right to blame that unknowing action?
      For my mother's marriage, how can you be so shameless,
      villain that you are, to make me speak of this?
      She was your sister. But what that marriage was
      I will say now. I will not hold my tongue,
      when you have gone so far in impious speech.
      She bore me, yes, she bore me—evil on evil—
1130 she knowing no more than I did, and having borne me
      brought forth, to her shame, those children to her son.
      One thing I do know: *you* know what you do,
      when you speak ill of her and me for this;
      but when I married her *I* did not know
      nor chose; nor, as I speak of it now,
      do I choose willingly to speak.

Even in this marriage I will not be reviled,
nor accept the bitter blame of father-killer
with which you have belabored me incessantly.
Answer me only one of my questions—this one.   1140
If someone here and now should stand beside you
trying to kill you—such a just man as you!—
would you ask the would-be killer was he your father,
or would you pay him back for the blow at once?
I think you would, if you love your life, pay back
the man who did it; you would not look around for
    justice.
Into such evil I entered, for the gods
guided me to it. I do not think
that my father's spirit, alive, would gainsay that.
But you, you are no just man—you think it right   1150
to say everything, things not to be spoken,
as well as those proper to speech; you taunt me
before these people here. You speak flatteringly
of Theseus' glorious name.
You say how nobly Athens is administered.
With all your lavish praise you forget this:
that if there is a land that understands
how to worship the gods in honor, this land excels.
This is the city, I am the suppliant, old,
and you tried to steal me from it; you laid your hands   1160
upon my daughters and made off with them.
For these your actions I call upon these Goddesses,
I beseech them, I entreat them with my prayers
to come as helpers and allies; so you shall learn
indeed what sort of government guards this city.

CHORUS: My lord the stranger is a good man; what has
        happened to him
    is all in all destructive; we should help him.

THESEUS: We have talked enough; those who have done
    this deed
  are hurrying away, while we the victims stand here.

1170 CREON: What would you have me do? I am quite helpless.

THESEUS: I want you to lead the way on their tracks, and I
    must go as your escort; if you have these girls
  still in my country, you may show them to me yourself.
  If those who have them are in flight, we may spare our
    trouble,
  for we have others to chase them. They will not escape
  and fleeing from this country bless their gods for it!
  Lead the way, you. Know, the taker is taken.
  You were the hunter; Fortune has hunted you down.
  What is gained by craft, unjustly, is not kept safely.
1180 You need not look for anyone else to help you—
  for I am sure that you were not alone
  nor unprovided, seeing that you have reached
  such recklessness and daring.
  You must have some accomplice in whom you trusted.
  I must look to all of this, nor make my city
  weaker than a single man. Do you understand
  anything of all this? Or are my words spoken in vain
  as those were that were said to you when you planned
    this act?

CREON: I will not fault anything you say to me
1190 when I am here. At home they will know what to do.

THESEUS: Threaten—but go on! For you, Oedipus,
  stay here at your ease, with absolute confidence
  that if I do not die first, I will not rest
  until I make your children yours again.

OEDIPUS: God bless you, Theseus, for your nobleness
  and for the justice of your care for me!

CHORUS: I would I were where the wheeling charge
of foemen soon will join
in fight to the clash of bronze,
on Pythian shores or the torch-lighted strand   1200
where the Sacred Ones cherish
their solemn rites for mortal men,
on whose tongues the golden key rested
of the ministrant Eumolpidae.

There, I think, they shall reunite—
our Theseus, rouser of battles,
and the two captive sister maids,
in the midst of the warring of men strong to
     save,
still within Attic bounds.

But perhaps it is where they approach   1210
the pastures of the west
of Oea's rock, snow-clad,
the prisoners riding or carried in chariots,
pushed to racing speed.

Creon will lose. Terrible is the might
of those that neighbor Colonus,
and terrible the might
of Theseus' folk.
Every bit shines, like a lightning flash.
Each horseman in eagerness rides,   1220
with loosened bridle rein.
They are the horsemen who honor
Athene, goddess of horsemanship,
and the Sea Lord, Earth shaker,
dear son of Rhea.
Is the action started, or yet to come?
My mind gives me hints of hope
soon again to see the two girls
so cruelly tried,

1230   so cruelly suffering
           at the hands of their kinfolk.
           Zeus will bring something to pass;
           he will—and on this day.
           I am the prophet
           of happy outcome.
           I would I were a dove in the sky,
           quick of wing,
           to reach a cloud over the fight
           with eyes lifted above the fight.

1240   O supreme ruler of Gods,
           Zeus who sees everything,
           grant that those who hold this land
           may achieve triumph, may win the prize
           with strength victorious.

           Holy daughter of Zeus,
           Pallas Athene, grant it,
           and you Apollo, the hunter,
           and your sister, the follower
           of dappled deer. I beg you
1250   for help to come doubly—
           for this land and for its citizens.

      Stranger and wanderer, you will not say
      that I who watched on your behalf
      was a false prophet. For I see
      the girls returning here, and escorted, too.

   OEDIPUS: Where? Where? What are you saying? How can
       it be?

   ANTIGONE: Father, O father! that some god would grant
       you
       to see this noble man who brought us home!

OEDIPUS: My dear, are you both here?

ANTIGONE: Yes, for the hands   1260
  of Theseus and his dear servants rescued us.

OEDIPUS: Come to your father, child, and let me touch
  that body I never hoped would come again!

ANTIGONE: You shall have your wish. What you beg of us
  is all our longing, too.

OEDIPUS: Where, oh where are you?

ANTIGONE: Here, we are right beside you.

OEDIPUS: Dear children!

ANTIGONE: All a father's love is there.

OEDIPUS: You loves, that have supported me!   1270

ANTIGONE: Poor daughters, and poor father!

OEDIPUS: I have what I love most. Where I still to die
    now,
  I would not be wholly wretched,
  for now I have you two beside me.
  Press on me, you on this side, you on that,
  clinging to your father; rest yourselves now
  from all the old wandering, lonely and unhappy.
  And tell me, but as shortly as you can
  what has happened. For girls like you
  a short tale suffices.   1280

ANTIGONE: Here is the man who rescued us. Hear him,
    father.
  He did it all—so shall my telling
  be brief enough.

OEDIPUS: Sir, do not wonder that with seeming obstinacy
    I prolong this conversation with my children;
    so utterly unexpected is what has happened!
    But I know well that from none else than you
    my joy in these has come to pass. You, you
    it is that saved me, you and no other man.
1290   May the gods grant all that I wish for you,
    for you and for this country! Only in this people
    of yours have I found piety towards the gods,
    and human feeling and no hypocrisy.
    I know all this—and with these words alone
    do I requite what you have done. I have
    all that I have through you and no one else.
    My lord, reach me your right hand; let me touch it
    and let me kiss your head—if that is lawful.

    What am I saying? How can a wretched being,
1300   such as I have become, wish to touch *you*,
    a man in whom no single stain of evil
    has dwelling place? I and you cannot do so.
    Nor will I suffer it to be. The possibility
    of sharing in my misery is only
    for those already in it.
    Stand where you are. God bless you where you stand!
    In the days to come may you look after me
    with the justice you have shown me in this hour!

THESEUS: Even if you had extended your words longer,
    I would not have wondered—for your delight in your
1310   children.
    Nor would I, if you preferred their words to mine.
    I have no weight of vexation at that.
    I would have my life one of distinction,
    not so much in words—rather by deeds achieved.
    I let you see that what I swore to you
    old man, I have not proved false to—not in anything.

For here I come, bringing your girls with me,
alive, untouched by all the threats against them.
How the fight was won, why should I boast pointlessly?
You yourself from these two will know all.   1320

But there *is* something of question that has happened to
     me
as I came here; let me have your counsel on it.
It is little to tell, but remarkable. No man
should treat of anything as insignificant.

OEDIPUS: What is it, son of Aegeus? Tell me.
I do not know what it is you ask about.

THESEUS: They say there is a man, no countryman
of yours, but of your kinfolk,
who had, it would seem, thrown himself down before
the altar of Poseidon, has taken his station there. It was   1330
where I was sacrificing, when I came here to you.

OEDIPUS: What countryman is he? What does he want,
that he sits there as suppliant?

THESEUS: I only know one thing.
He asks some little speech with you. This is no great
     matter.

OEDIPUS: What can it be? His suppliant seat there does not
suggest some trivial matter.

THESEUS: What they say
is that he asks only to talk with you
and go away without suffering for coming here.   1340

OEDIPUS: Who can he be that makes this supplication?

THESEUS: Reflect if there be anyone in Argos
akin to you, that he might ask this favor.

OEDIPUS: Dearest of friends, stop right where you are!

THESEUS: What is it?

OEDIPUS: Do not beg this of me.

THESEUS: What is it, that I should not?

OEDIPUS: As I hear you, I know who this suppliant is.

THESEUS: And who is he that I should find fault with him?

1350   OEDIPUS: He is my son, prince, he is my hated son,
        whose words would hurt my ears more than all others.

THESEUS: What is this? Surely it's possible
        to listen and not do what you do not want?
        Why should it be so bitter to you to *hear* him?

OEDIPUS: His voice, prince, has become a thing most
        hateful
        to me his father; do not constrain me
        to yield in this.

THESEUS: Consider if it be not his suppliancy
        that makes your yielding a necessity.
1360   Perhaps regard for the god should make you careful.

ANTIGONE: Father, let me persuade you, though I am
        young to advise.
        Suffer the king here to gratify his own heart
        and give the god what the prince would have you give
        him.
        For our sake (*pointing to her sister*), suffer our brother to
        come here.
        He will not tear you from your resolution—
        do not fear that—if he pleads what is unfit.
        What harm is there in hearing what he says?
        Evil contrivings are best revealed in speech.
        You begot him; even if what he does to you
1370   is the most impious of all that is vile,

you ought not, father, to match him in evil.
No, let him come. Other men have had bad sons,
and have had sharp tempers.
But when they were schooled by friends' enchanting
      voices
their natures yield to the might of them. You,
look to that other time—not now—
the father-and-mother evils that you suffered.
If you look at that other time, I am sure,
you will know the evil end of anger, the evil
which comes to climax in it. What your heart tells you
      then   1380
are not slight things—when you lost those eyes, now
      sightless.
Yield to us all; it is not right
that those who ask what is just should have to be
importunate; nor that the man himself
who has had good treatment should not know how
to pay requital for it.

OEDIPUS: My child, when you win me with your words,
    it is a bitter pleasure to yield. Let it be so,
    as you will have it. Only, sir, if he comes here
    let no one have the disposal of my life.   1390

THESEUS: Once is enough for that. I do not need to hear
      it twice,
    old man; I do not want to boast, but you,
    you know you are safe—if a god keeps *me* safe.

CHORUS: Whoever it is that seeks to have
        a greater share of life,
        letting moderation slip out of his thoughts,
        I count him a fool, a persistent fool;
        I am clear in my mind of that.

Indeed, the long days store up many things
1400   that are nearer to sorrow than joy,
and the whereabouts of delight
you will not find, once you have fallen
into the region beyond your due term.
The Helper still is the same for all,
the same Consummator,
Death at the last,
the appearance of Death in Doom.
He comes to no sound of wedding joy,
no lyre, no dances.

1410   Not to be born is best of all;
when life is there, the second best
to go hence where you came,
with the best speed you may.
For when his youth with its gift of light heart
has come and gone, what grievous stroke
is spared to a man, what agony
is he without? Envy, and faction,
strife and fighting and murders are his,
and yet there is something more that claims him,
1420   old age at the last, most hated,
without power, without comrades, and friends,
when every ill, all ills,
take up their dwelling with him.
So, he is old—this old man here—
I am not alone in that,
as the wave-lashed cape that faces north,
in the wintertime,
the din of the winds on every side,
the din of the mischiefs encompass him utterly,
1430   like the breaking crests of the waves forever,
some from the setting sun,
some from his rising,

and some from the place of his midday beams,
and some from the northern mountains of night.

ANTIGONE: Here he is, it seems, this stranger,
alone, my father, weeping his tears in floods,
as he comes here.

OEDIPUS: Who is it?

ANTIGONE: He whom we always held in
mind
that it would be; here is Polyneices.   1440

POLYNEICES: O, what shall I do?
Shall I cry for my own troubles, first of all,
my sisters? Or his, my old father's,
as I see them before me?
Here I find him in a foreign country,
an exile banished here, with clothes upon him
where the foul ancient dirt has lived so long
that it infects his old body,
and his uncombed hair floats in the wind
about his eyeless face.   1450
The food he carries to fill his belly,
is, I should guess, akin to what he wears.
I learn all this too late, wretch that I am!
I will bear witness against myself, as the world's villain,
for not supporting him. You need not learn
from others what I am.
But yet there is Mercy; in everything
she shares the throne of Zeus. Let her stand by you
too, father. Why are you silent?
Say something!   1460
Do not turn away from me giving no answer,
sending me hence dishonored by your silence,
not even telling me why you are angry.
You children of this father, blood of my blood,
will you try at least to make him open his mouth

that now denies approach, in implacable silence?
So may he not dismiss me in dishonor—
a god's suppliant that I am—with never a word.

ANTIGONE: Speak yourself, unhappy man, say what you
    come to seek.
1470   The flood of words may give some kind of pleasure:
They may make angry or just bring some pity;
still, somehow, they give a voice to what is voiceless.

POLYNEICES: Then I will speak; your advice is good.
First, here I make the god my helper
from whose altar the prince of this country raised me up
to come to you. He granted me permission
to speak, and hear, and a safe-conduct home.
These things I would have from you, my foreign friends,
and from my sisters and my father.
1480   Father, I want to tell you why I came here.
I have been banished from my country, made an exile,
because I claimed my right as the elder born
to sit upon your sovereign throne. For this,
my younger brother, Eteocles, drove me out.
He did not have the best of me in words,
nor in the proof of hand or deed. It was the city
which he persuaded. The chief reason, I think,
was the curse, *your* curse, that lay upon the house.
That is what I hear also from the soothsayers.

1490   When I came to the Dorian land of Argos
Adrastus gave me his daughter to wife.
Then I swore to my side all
that were reputed best and honored most
for skill in warfare in the Apian land,
that I might gather from these a seven-fold band
of spearmen against Thebes; then with justice on my side
either die—or banish those that had done me wrong.

Very well, then; why have I come to you?
To bring, my father, my suppliant prayers, for myself
and for my allies, who with seven hosts   1500
behind their seven spears encompass about
the entire plain of Thebes.

There is the spearman, Amphiareus, supreme
master in war, supreme in knowledge of omens;
the second is the Aetolian, son of Oeneus,
Tydeus; third Eteoclus, born an Argive;
the fourth Hippomedon, sent by his father Talaos;
the fifth Capaneus, who has vowed to burn
the city of Thebes into the ground; the sixth
Parthenopaeus, the Arcadian, hastens to the war,   1510
his name recalling his mother, long a virgin
but brought at last to travail by the trusty
son of Atlanta;
and then myself, yours but not yours, begotten
of an evil fate, yet called at least your son,
I lead the fearless host of Argos to Thebes.

We all entreat you, by these your children, by
your life, my father, remit your heavy anger
against me, as I set forth to punish my brother
who thrust me out, despoiled me of my country.   1520
For if there is any trust to be placed in oracles,
they have said the victory shall come to those
whose side you join.
Then, by our fountains, and our race's gods,
I beg you to be persuaded and to yield.
We are beggars and foreigners both—and so are you!
We live by flattering others, both you and I.
We have drawn the selfsame lot in life.
But he is a prince, at home—oh wretched me!—
and laughs at both of us, in luxury.   1530
If you will stand a helper to my purpose

I will shake him out of it with little trouble
and quick enough, so that I can place you again
in your own house and place myself there too,
once I have driven him out and forcefully.
I may make this my boast if you stand by me,
without you I have no strength, even to survive.

CHORUS: Oedipus, as to this man,
    out of consideration for him that sent him here,
1540   say what is proper and send him on his way.

OEDIPUS: Yes, public guardians of this land, I will.
    If he that sent him to me had not been
    Theseus, who thought it right that he should hear
    words of mine, he never would have heard my voice.
    But now he will go hence, having been thought worthy
    and heard from me such words as never will
    gladden his life.
    You scoundrel, you, with your scepter and your
        throne—
    held now by your blood brother in Thebes—
1550   you chased me out, your father, made me cityless;
    these are the clothes *you* made me wear,
    the sight of which now brings tears to your eyes,
    when *you* have come to the same stress of misery.
    I may not weep, *I* must put up with it
    as long as I live remembering my murderer;
    you have contrived my rearing in agony;
    you drove me out. It is because of you
    I am a wanderer begging my daily bread.
    Had I not begotten these children to be my nurses
1560   I had been dead, for all you did to help.
    Now it is they who save me, these very nurses.
    They are men, not women, in bearing troubles with me.
    You are no sons of mine, you are someone else's.
    Therefore the Evil Spirit has eyes upon you,

although, by and by, those eyes will be still fiercer,
if these hosts are really moving towards Thebes.
That city you will not destroy—no, before that
you will fall yourself, polluted with blood, and equally
your brother. Such are the curses I sent forth
in days gone by, against you two. And now   1570
I summon those curses to come to me as allies,
that you two, brothers, may know to reverence parents,
and not dishonor a father because he was blind—
and got such men as you for sons. These girls
have done none of this.
Therefore my curses overcome
your suppliant seat, and that, your throne, in Thebes,
as sure as Justice, claimed of old time, is sharer
in Zeus' throne, by the might of the old laws.
Get you gone! I spit you from me. I am no father   1580
of yours, you worst of villains! Pack away
all of these curses that I invoke against you.
You shall not conquer by spear your native land:
you shall not come again to hollow Argos;
you are to die by a brother's hand, and kill him
by whom you were exiled.
There are my curses on you! And I summon
your father's hateful darkness of Tartarus
to give you a new dwelling place. I call
upon the spirits there, I call on Ares,   1590
that thrust upon you both this dreadful hatred.

That is what you have heard. Now, off with you and tell
all the Cadmeans and your trusty allies
that such are the honors Oedipus divided
between those sons of his!

CHORUS: I had no pleasure, Polyneices,
     in your past journeyings. Now, speedily back again!

POLYNEICES: Woe for my journey! woe for its ill success!
Woe for my comrades! what an end this road had
1600   when we set out from Argos! woe is me!
such an end that I cannot tell to any
of those comrades, nor yet turn *them* home again!
but, saying nothing, go on to meet my fortune.
Sisters—for you *are* my sisters, although his daughters—
since you have heard my father's dreadful curses,
I pray you two, by the gods, if the day come
when his curses come to pass, and you have somehow
come home again, do not dishonor me,
but lay me in a grave with funeral rites.
1610   You have praise now, for the pains that you took,
in caring for this old man; you will earn no less
besides for helping me.

ANTIGONE: Polyneices, I entreat you,
do the thing that I ask you.

POLYNEICES: Dearest Antigone,
what is it? Tell me.

ANTIGONE: Turn your army
back to Argos speedily. Do not
destroy yourself and the city both.

1620   POLYNEICES: I cannot
do this. How can I lead this selfsame army
back again when I have once
proved myself coward?

ANTIGONE: Why must you, brother, fall to anger again?
If you destroy your own country, what do you gain?

POLYNEICES: Exile is shameful, and shameful that one
elder
be so mocked by his brother.

ANTIGONE: Do you see, then,
    how right our father's prophecies come out
    when he spoke of the mutual murder of you two?   1630

POLYNEICES: That is what *he* wants. But I must not yield.

ANTIGONE: Wretched that I am! But who, once he has
        heard
    our father's prophecies, will dare to follow you?

POLYNEICES: I will not tell bad news. That is good
        generalship—
    to tell one's strengths and not one's weaknesses.

ANTIGONE: Then, brother, you are truly so determined?

POLYNEICES: Do not stop me. Now this must be my care,
    this road of mine, ill-omened and terrible,
    made so by my father and those Furies of his;
    but may Zeus prosper *your* road, if you fulfill   1640
    my wishes, at my death. For me in life
    there is nothing you can do. Let me go now,
    and, both of you, goodbye. You will never again
    see me alive.

ANTIGONE: My heart is broken!

POLYNEICES: Do not mourn for me.

ANTIGONE: Brother, how can anyone
    not mourn, seeing you set out
    to death so clear before you?

POLYNEICES: If die I must, I'll die.   1650

ANTIGONE: Do not, dearest;
    do as I say.

POLYNEICES: Do not try to persuade me
    to fail my duty.

ANTIGONE: Then I am utterly
destroyed if I must lose you.

POLYNEICES: All of that
whether for good or ill, Fortune determines.
But for you two, I pray the gods that never
1660   you meet with ill. In all men's judgment
you should not suffer misfortune.

CHORUS: Here are other new ills that have come
just now, of evil doom,
from the blind stranger—
unless Fate is somehow at work.
For I cannot call any decision of God
a vain thing.
Time watches constantly those decisions;
Some fortunes it destroys, and others,
1670   on the day following, lifts up again.

There is the thunder! Zeus!

OEDIPUS: My children, children, please can someone go
and fetch for me Theseus that best of men?

ANTIGONE: Father, what is the occasion of your summons?

OEDIPUS: The winged thunder of Zeus will carry me
straightway to death. Send and send quickly!

CHORUS: Look at it! rolling down, crashing,
the thunderbolt unspeakable, hurled by Zeus.
Terror has raised the hair on my head;
1680   my heart is trembling.
There, again, is the flash of the lightning!
It burns in the sky. What event will it yield?
I am all fear. It is not for nothing
when it lightens so; there will be issue of it.
O, the great sky! O Zeus!

OEDIPUS: Children, there has come to me, as the gods said,
my end of life. There is no more turning away.

ANTIGONE: How do you know? What makes you think it?

OEDIPUS: I know it well. But, quickly, someone go
and summon here this country's prince. 1690

CHORUS: See, there again, around us
the piercing thunder!
Be merciful, God, if you are bringing
some black-night thing
to this land, our mother.
May I find you gracious.
Because I have looked on a man accursed
may I not have a share in a graceless grace!
Lord Zeus, to you I cry.

OEDIPUS: Is the man near? And children, will he find me 1700
still alive and my wits not astray?

ANTIGONE: What confidence would you implant in his
mind?

OEDIPUS: That, for the kindness he has shown me, the
requital,
as I once promised, now is duly paid.

CHORUS: My son, come here,
or if in the innermost recess of the glade
you are hallowing Poseidon's altar
with sacrifice of cattle, come still.
For the stranger claims to make return
to you, and the city and his friends, 1710
a just return for a just kindness done.

THESEUS: What is this public summons from all of you,
clearly from my people, clearly from this stranger?

Is it the thunder of Zeus or rushing hail?
One can indeed conjecture anything
when Zeus sends such a storm.

OEDIPUS: My lord, I have longed for you and you have
        come.
    Some god has made for you a happy blessing
    from this coming.

1720   THESEUS: What new thing is it, son of Laius?

OEDIPUS: The balance of my life's scale has come down.
    I will not choose to fail my promises
    to you and the city, now, before I die.

THESEUS: What evidence have you of this impending
        death?

OEDIPUS: The gods are their own messengers to me;
    they are not false to the signs they have arranged.

THESEUS: What signs? Make this clear, old man.

OEDIPUS: The long continued thunder, the massive
        lightning
    hurled from the hand that never knew defeat.

1730   THESEUS: I believe you; for I have seen you prophesy
        much, and falsely never. Tell me what to do.

OEDIPUS: Yes; I will direct you, son of Aegeus,
    in what shall be a treasure for this city.
    Old age shall not decay it. Immediately
    I will show the way without a hand to guide me
    to the place where I must die.
    And you, describe this to no man, ever,
    neither where it is hidden nor in what region,
    that doing so may make you a defense
    beyond the worth of many shields, or many neighbors'
1740   help.

The things within this ban, not to be uttered,
yourself shall learn, when you come there alone,
for I shall not declare them to anyone
of these citizens, nor to my daughters, dear though I
    hold them.
Keep them yourself always, and when you come
to the end of life reveal them only
to him that is nearest to you, and he in turn
to his successor.
So you shall hold this city undevastated
by the Sown Men. Ten thousand states   1750
have committed violence on one another,
despite their rulers' excellent government.
For the gods are careful watchers at the last
but slow in action, when one dismissing gods' will
has turned to madness. Never
let that befall you, son of Aegeus.
But I will not school you in such things; you know
    them.
Let us now go to the place—a pressing summons
from the god forces me—and delay no more.
My children, follow me—so. In a strange way   1760
I have become your guide; you were once mine.
Come on, but touch me not. Suffer me to find
my sacred grave where it is fated
that I shall be hidden in this country's earth.
This way, this way, like this! For this way Hermes,
the Conductor, leads me, and the goddess of the dead.
O light, no light though you were once a light
to me! now for the last time touch my body.
For I creep along to hide my last of life
in Hades. You dearest of friends (*to Theseus*)   1770
yourself, this land and these your citizens—
blessings upon you! and in your blessedness
remember me, the dead! Live blessed forever.

CHORUS: If it be lawful, it is mine
              to adore with prayers the Goddess Unseen
              and you, my lord of the Creatures of Night,
              Aidoneus, Aidoneus,
              that our stranger friend may pass to his end
              untroubled and free of the tears

1780   attendant on a grievous doom;
              that he may come to the world below,
              that hides all within itself,
              to the land of the dead, the Stygian house.
              Many the ills that were his, all uncalled for;
              may God in justice exalt him again!

              O goddesses of that Underworld,
              and Form of the Hound Unconquered
              who keeps his lair at the guest-haunted gate,
              and sleeps and snuffles from out his cave,

1790   the guardian in death's house, unsubdued—
              thus is always the story told.

              O son of Earth and Tartarus
              I pray that that Hound may give a clear path
              to our friend coming down
              to dead men's country;
              You, Giver of Sleep Everlasting,
              I call on You.

MESSENGER: Citizens: to speak most briefly and truthfully,
          Oedipus is gone. But what has happened,

1800   the tale of that cannot be told so briefly,
          for the acts there were not brief.

CHORUS: The unhappy man is gone!

MESSENGER: You must think of him
          as of one truly parted out of life.

CHORUS: How was it? By God's chance and painlessly
  the poor man ended?

MESSENGER: That is wonderful indeed.
  How he moved from here with no guidance of friends,
  you yourselves know. For I think you were here.
  He was himself the guide to all of us.   1810
  When he came to the steep road, rooted in earth
  by brazen steps, he stood in one of the many
  branching paths, near the hollow basin
  where is, forever confident, the memorial
  to Theseus' and Peirithous' compact.
  Where he stood, he was midway between
  that basin and the Thorician rock,
  the hollow pear tree and the grave of stone.

  Then he sat down and loosed his filthy robes,
  cried loudly to his daughters to bring him water   1820
  from some stream, to wash and make drink offerings.
  They hurried to Demeter's hill, in front of them,
  guardian of tender plants; they brought what he ordered;
  and then with lustral washing and with clothes
  equipped him in the customary fashion.
  When he had his pleasure of all he did,
  and nothing that he sought was scanted, Zeus
  of the Underworld thundered. They fell at their father's
      knees
  and cried, ceaselessly, beating their breasts,
  and with unending long laments. But he,   1830
  when he heard the sudden bitter cries from them,
  folded his hands upon them; then said "My children,
  this is the day when you become fatherless.
  All that was me has perished; now no more
  for you the heavy task of tending me.
  It was a cruel task, children, that I know,
  but there's a single word that overthrows

all tasks of work. My love you had; no one
could love you more. That is the love you lose now
1840   and must pass through the rest of life without it."
They embraced and sobbed shrilly, all three of them.
When they came to the end of their mourning
and not another cry rose, there, in the stillness,
there was a voice of someone, summoning him,
and suddenly in their terror, all hair stood up.
It was the god who called him, over and over,
"You, Oedipus, Oedipus, why are you hesitating
to go our way? You have been too slow, too long."
When he understood that calling of the god,
1850   he cried to this country's ruler, Theseus,
to come to him, and when he came, he said:
"You that I love, give me your hand's sworn pledge
to these my children, and you, my children, to him.
Promise me that you will never consciously
forsake them, but perform whatever you judge
will be for their advantage always."
He, noble man that he is, gave him his promise
and with no word of sorrow swore he would do
that, for his friend.
1860   When he had finished, suddenly Oedipus
touching his children with blind hands said "Both, my
          children,
be brave and noble of mind, and leave this place.
Do not seek to know what is forbidden,
nor hear it from others' speaking.
Quickly, away with you; only let Theseus
stay to understand what is to be done."

That was what he said; we listened all,
and with the girls in tears and lamentations,
followed them away. When we departed,
1870   in a few moments we looked back and saw that

Oedipus, yes, Oedipus, was no longer there,
but the king by himself, holding his hand
before his face, to shade his eyes, as though
some deadly terror had appeared to him
that sight could not endure.
Then just a little afterwards, we saw him
bow to salute the earth and the gods' Olympus
united in the same prayer at once.
But by what manner of doom that other died
no mortal man can say, save our lord Theseus.   1880
It was no fiery thunderbolt of God
that made away with him, nor a sea hurricane
rising; no, it was some messenger
sent by the gods, or some power of the dead
split open the fundament of earth, with good will,
to give him painless entry. He was sent on his way
with no accompaniment of tears, no pain of sickness;
if any man ended miraculously,
this man did. If I seem to talk nonsense,
I would not try to win over such as think so.   1890

CHORUS: Where are the girls? And where their escorting
    friends?

MESSENGER: Not far away. The sounds of their mourning
    voices
show they are coming here.

ANTIGONE: Now it belongs to both of us,
    unhappy beings, to sorrow
    for the curse that inheres
    in our father's blood;
    not for this part, yes, and for that part, no—
    totally.
    For him we have borne in his life   1900
    a great burden unrelieved,

but now at the end we will have to speak
of things beyond reason's scope,
what we saw, what we suffered.

CHORUS: What is it?

ANTIGONE: My friends, we can only guess.

CHORUS: He has gone?

ANTIGONE: As you would have him go.
        What else can be said of one
1910   whom neither the War God,
        nor the sea encountered,
        but the unseen fields of the world of Death
        snatched away in some doom invisible?
        On us two destruction's night
        has settled on our eyes.
        How shall we wander, how find
        a bitter living in distant lands
        or on the waves of the sea?

ISMENE: I do not know.
1920   Let murdering Hades
        take me and join me in death with him,
        my father in his old age.
        The life that will henceforth be mine
        is a life that cannot be lived.

CHORUS: You two are the best of children;
        you must bear what the god gives to bear.
        No more fire of grief. You cannot truly
        sorrow for what has happened.

ANTIGONE: There can be a love
1930   even of suffering;
        for that which is anything but dear itself
        could still be dear,

while I still had him in these hands of mine.
Father, dear one, you that forever
have put on the darkness of underground,
even there you shall not be unloved,
by me and by my sister.

CHORUS: His end?

ANTIGONE: His end is what he wished.

CHORUS: What end? 1940

ANTIGONE: And he died in a foreign land,
but one he yearned for. He has his bed
below in the shadowy grass
forever.
He has left behind him a mourning sorrow—
these eyes of mine with their tears
bewail you. I do not know how
in my misery I should cast out
such a weight of sorrow.
Yes, you chose in a foreign land 1950
to die. I find it a lonely death.

ISMENE: What further destiny awaits
you and me, dear one, alone as we are?

CHORUS: My dears, the end of his life was blessed;
do not keep sorrowing. No one
is hard for misfortune to capture.

ANTIGONE: Let us hurry back, sister.

ISMENE: What to do?

ANTIGONE: Desire possesses me—

ISMENE: What desire? 1960

ANTIGONE: To see where he lies in earth.

ISMENE: Who lies?

ANTIGONE: Our father—Oh, misery!

ISMENE: How can that be lawful?
  Do you not see?

ANTIGONE: Why do you blame me for this?

ISMENE: And this again—

ANTIGONE: What is *this* again?

ISMENE: Where he fell, there *is* no grave—
1970   and he was quite alone.

ANTIGONE: Bring me where he was,
  and then kill me.

ISMENE: Where now so lonely,
  so helpless, shall *I* live?

CHORUS: Friends, do not be afraid!

ANTIGONE: But where to find refuge?

CHORUS: You *have* found refuge.

ANTIGONE: From what?

CHORUS: From misfortune, refuge for you both.

1980 ANTIGONE: I understand.

CHORUS: What is it you are thinking?

ANTIGONE: I cannot tell
  how I can come home.

CHORUS: Do not seek to go home.

ANTIGONE: Trouble is upon us.

CHORUS: It has pursued you before.

ANTIGONE: Desperate then, but now still worse.

CHORUS: Yes, yours was a sea of sorrow.

ANTIGONE: Where shall we go, O God?
   To what of hope now 1990
   can Fate drive us?
(*Theseus enters.*)

THESEUS: Cease your mourning, children; for those
   to whom the grace of the Underworld Gods
   has been stored as a treasure, to the quick and the dead,
   for them there shall be no mourning.
   Else the gods may be angry.

ANTIGONE: Son of Aegeus, we beg you—

THESEUS: What would you have me grant, children?

ANTIGONE: We would ourselves see the grave
   of our father. 2000

THESEUS: No, this is not lawful.

ANTIGONE: What do you mean, king of Athens?

THESEUS: He
   has forbidden approach to the place,
   nor may any voice invoke
   the sacred tomb where he lies.
   He said, if I truly did this,
   I should have forever a land unharmed.
   These pledges the God heard from me
   and Oath, Zeus' servant, all seeing. 2010

ANTIGONE: If this was, then, the mind of Him,
   the dead, I must be content.
   Send us, then, to our ancient Thebes
   that perhaps we may prevent
   the murder that comes to our brothers.

THESEUS: That I will do and whatever else
shall profit yourselves and pleasure both you
and the man under earth who is newly gone—
for him I must spare no pains.

2020 CHORUS: Now cease lamentation, nor further prolong
your dirge. All of these matters
have found their consummation.

ANTIGONE

CHARACTERS

ANTIGONE
ISMENE
CHORUS OF THEBAN ELDERS
CREON
A SENTRY
HAEMON
TEIRESIAS
A MESSENGER
EURYDICE
SECOND MESSENGER

ANTIGONE

*(The two sisters Antigone and Ismene meet in front of
the palace gates in Thebes.)*

*[handwritten: Bringing in from palace
guards surrendery
must be quiet]*

ANTIGONE: Ismene, my dear sister,
 whose father was my father, can you think of any
 of all the evils that stem from Oedipus
 that Zeus does not bring to pass for us, while we yet
  live?
 No pain, no ruin, no shame, and no dishonor
 but I have seen it in our mischiefs,
 yours and mine.
 And now what is the proclamation that they tell of
 made lately by the commander, publicly,
 to all the people? Do you know it? Have you heard it?   10
 Don't you notice when the evils due to enemies
 are headed towards those we love?

ISMENE: Not a word, Antigone, of those we love,
 either sweet or bitter, has come to me since the moment
 when we lost our two brothers,
 on one day, by their hands dealing mutual death.
 Since the Argive army fled in this past night,
 I know of nothing further, nothing
 of better fortune or of more destruction.

ANTIGONE: *I* knew it well; that is why I sent for you   20
 to come outside the palace gates   *[handwritten: explain why were outside]*
 to listen to me, privately.

ISMENE: What is it? Certainly your words
 come of dark thoughts.

ANTIGONE: Yes, indeed; for those two brothers of ours,
    in burial
  has not Creon honored the one, dishonored
    the other?
  Eteocles, they say he has used justly
  with lawful rites and hid him in the earth
  to have his honor among the dead men there.
30 But the unhappy corpse of Polyneices
  he has proclaimed to all the citizens,
  they say, no man may hide
  in a grave nor mourn in funeral,
  but leave unwept, unburied, a dainty treasure
  for the birds that see him, for their feast's delight.
  That is what, they say, the worthy Creon
  has proclaimed for you and me—for me, I tell you—
  and he comes here to clarify to the unknowing
  his proclamation; he takes it seriously;
40 for whoever breaks the edict death is prescribed,
  and death by stoning publicly.
  There you have it; soon you will show yourself
  as noble both in your nature and your birth,
  or yourself as base, although of noble parents.

ISMENE: If things are as you say, poor sister, how
  can I better them? how loose or tie the knot?

ANTIGONE: Decide if you will share the work, the deed.

ISMENE: What kind of danger is there? How far have
  your thoughts gone?

ANTIGONE: Here is this hand. Will you help it to lift the
  dead man?

50 ISMENE: Would you bury him, when it is forbidden the
  city?

ANTIGONE: At least he is my brother—and yours, too,
  though you deny him. *I* will not prove false to him.

ISMENE: You are so headstrong. Creon has forbidden it.

ANTIGONE: It is not for him to keep me from my own.

ISMENE: O God!
  Consider, sister, how our father died,
  hated and infamous; how he brought to light
  his own offenses; how he himself struck out
  the sight of his two eyes;
  his own hand was their executioner.   60
  Then, mother and wife, two names in one, did shame
  violently on her life, with twisted cords.
  Third, our two brothers, on a single day,
  poor wretches, themselves worked out their mutual
    doom.
  Each killed the other, hand against brother's hand.
  Now there are only the two of us, left behind,
  and see how miserable our end shall be
  if in the teeth of law we shall transgress
  against the sovereign's decree and power.
  You ought to realize we are only women,   70
  not meant in nature to fight against men,
  and that we are ruled, by those who are stronger,
  to obedience in this and even more painful matters.
  I do indeed beg those beneath the earth
  to give me their forgiveness,
  since force constrains me,
  that I shall yield in this to the authorities.
  Extravagant action is not sensible.

ANTIGONE: I would not urge you now; nor if you wanted
  to act would I be glad to have you with me.   80
  Be as you choose to be; but for myself
  I myself will bury him. It will be good
  to die, so doing. I shall lie by his side,
  loving him as he loved me; I shall be

a criminal—but a religious one.
The time in which I must please those that are dead
is longer than I must please those of this world.
For there I shall lie forever. You, if you like,
can cast dishonor on what the gods have honored.

90   ISMENE: I will not put dishonor on them, but
        to act in defiance of the citizenry,
        my nature does not give me means for that.

ANTIGONE: Let that be your excuse. But I will go
        to heap the earth on the grave of my loved brother.

ISMENE: How I fear for you, my poor sister!

ANTIGONE: Do not fear for me. Make straight your own
        path to destiny.

ISMENE: At least do not speak of this act to anyone else;
        bury him in secret; I will be silent, too.

ANTIGONE: Oh, oh, no! shout it out. I will hate you still
        worse
100   for silence—should you not proclaim it,
        to everyone.

ISMENE: You have a warm heart for such chilly deeds.

ANTIGONE: I know I am pleasing those I should please
        most.

ISMENE: If you can do it. But you are in love
        with the impossible.

ANTIGONE: No. When I can no more, then I will stop.

ISMENE: It is better not to hunt the impossible
        at all.

ANTIGONE: If you will talk like this I will loathe you,
110   and you will be adjudged an enemy—

justly—by the dead's decision. Let me alone
and my folly with me, to endure this terror.
No suffering of mine will be enough
to make me die ignobly.

ISMENE: Well, if you will, go on.
Know this; that though you are wrong to go, your
    friends
are right to love you.

CHORUS: Sun's beam, fairest of all
         that ever till now shone
         on seven-gated Thebes;   120
         O golden eye of day, you shone
         coming over Dirce's stream;
         you drove in headlong rout
         the whiteshielded man from Argos,
         complete in arms;
         his bits rang sharper
         under your urging.

         Polyneices brought him here
         against our land, Polyneices,
         roused by contentious quarrel;   130
         like an eagle he flew into our country,
         with many men-at-arms,
         with many a helmet crowned with horsehair.

         He stood above the halls, gaping with
                 murderous lances,
         encompassing the city's
         seven-gated mouth.
         But before his jaws would be sated
         with our blood, before the fire,
         pine fed, should capture our crown of towers,
         he went hence—   140
         such clamor of war stretched behind his back,
         from his dragon foe, a thing he could not
                 overcome.

For Zeus, who hates the most
the boasts of a great tongue,
saw them coming in a great tide,
insolent in the clang of golden armor.
The god struck him down with hurled fire,
as he strove to raise the victory cry,
now at the very winning post.

150   The earth rose to strike him as he fell swinging.
In his frantic onslaught, possessed, he breathed
         upon us
with blasting winds of hate.
Sometimes the great god of war was on one side,
and sometimes he struck a staggering blow on
         the other;
the god was a very wheel horse on the right
         trace.

At seven gates stood seven captains,
ranged equals against equals, and there left
their brazen suits of armor
to Zeus, the god of trophies.
Only those two wretches born of one father and
160   mother
set their spears to win a victory on both sides;
they worked out their share in a common death.

Now Victory, whose name is great, has come
to Thebes of many chariots
with joy to answer her joy,
to bring forgetfulness of these wars;
let us go to all the shrines of the gods
and dance all night long.
Let Bacchus lead the dance,
170   shaking Thebes to trembling.

But here is the king of our land,
Creon, son of Menoeceus;

in our new contingencies with the gods,
he is our new ruler.
He comes to set in motion some design—
what design is it? Because he has proposed
the convocation of the elders.
He sent a public summons for our discussion.

CREON: Gentlemen: as for our city's fortune,
the gods have shaken her, when the great waves broke,   180
but the gods have brought her through again to safety.
For yourselves, I chose you out of all and summoned
    you
to come to me, partly because I knew you
as always loyal to the throne—at first,
when Laius was king, and then again
when Oedipus saved our city and then again
when he died and you remained with steadfast truth
to their descendants,
until they met their double fate upon one day,
striking and stricken, defiled each by a brother's murder.   190
Now here I am, holding all authority
and the throne, in virtue of kinship with the dead.

It is impossible to know any man—
I mean his soul, intelligence, and judgment—
until he shows his skill in rule and law.
I think that a man supreme ruler of a whole city,
if he does not reach for the best counsel for her,
but through some fear, keeps his tongue under lock and
    key,
                                                            200
him I judge the worst of any;
I have always judged so; and anyone thinking
another man more a friend than his own country,
I rate him nowhere. For my part, God is my witness,
who sees all, always, I would not be silent
if I saw ruin, not safety, on the way

towards my fellow citizens. I would not count
any enemy of my country as a friend—
because of what I know, that she it is
which gives us our security. If she sails upright
and we sail on her, friends will be ours for the making.
In the light of rules like these, I will make her greater
210   still.

In consonance with this, I here proclaim
to the citizens about Oedipus' sons.
For Eteocles, who died this city's champion,
showing his valor's supremacy everywhere,
he shall be buried in his grave with every rite
of sanctity given to heroes under earth.
However, his brother, Polyneices, a returned exile,
who sought to burn with fire from top to bottom
his native city, and the gods of his own people;
220   who sought to taste the blood he shared with us,
and lead the rest of us to slavery—
I here proclaim to the city that this man
shall no one honor with a grave and none shall mourn.
You shall leave him without burial; you shall watch him
chewed up by birds and dogs and violated.
Such is my mind in the matter; never by me
shall the wicked man have precedence in honor
over the just. But he that is loyal to the state
in death, in life alike, shall have my honor.

230   CHORUS: Son of Menoeceus, so it is your pleasure
to deal with foe and friend of this our city.
To use any legal means lies in your power,
both about the dead and those of us who live.

CREON: I understand, then, you will do my bidding.

CHORUS: Please lay this burden on some younger man.

CREON: Oh, watchers of the corpse I have already.

CHORUS: What else, then, do your commands entail?

CREON: That you should not side with those who
disagree.

CHORUS: There is none so foolish as to love his own death.

CREON: Yes, indeed those are the wages, but often greed   240
has with its hopes brought men to ruin.

[*The sentry whose speeches follow represents a remarkable
experiment in Greek tragedy in the direction of naturalism of
speech. He speaks with marked clumsiness, partly because he is
excited and talks almost colloquially. But also the royal presence
makes him think apparently that he should be rather grand in his
show of respect. He uses odd bits of archaism or somewhat stale
poetical passages, particularly in catch phrases. He sounds
something like lower-level Shakespearean characters, e.g. Constable
Elbow, with his uncertainty about benefactor and malefactor.*]

SENTRY: My lord, I will never claim my shortness of
breath
is due to hurrying, nor were there wings in my feet.
I stopped at many a lay-by in my thinking;
I circled myself till I met myself coming back.
My soul accosted me with different speeches.
"Poor fool, yourself, why are you going somewhere
when once you get there you will pay the piper?"
"Well, aren't you the daring fellow! stopping again?
and suppose Creon hears the news from someone else—   250
don't you realize that you will smart for that?"
I turned the whole matter over. I suppose I may say
"I made haste slowly" and the short road became long.
However, at last I came to a resolve:
I must go to you; even if what I say
is nothing, really, still I shall say it.
I come here, a man with a firm clutch on the hope
that nothing can betide him save what is fated.

CREON: What is it then that makes you so afraid?

260 SENTRY: No, I want first of all to tell you my side of it.
I didn't do the thing; I never saw who did it.
It would not be fair for me to get into trouble.

CREON: You hedge, and barricade the thing itself.
Clearly you have some ugly news for me.

SENTRY: Well, you know how disasters make a man
hesitate to be their messenger.

CREON: For God's sake, tell me and get out of here!

SENTRY: Yes, I *will* tell you. Someone just now
buried the corpse and vanished. He scattered on the skin
270 some thirsty dust; he did the ritual,
duly, to purge the body of desecration.

CREON: What! Now who on earth could have done that?

SENTRY: I do not know. For there was there no mark
of axe's stroke nor casting up of earth
of any mattock; the ground was hard and dry,
unbroken; there were no signs of wagon wheels.
The doer of the deed had left no trace.
But when the first sentry of the day pointed it out,
there was for all of us a disagreeable
280 wonder. For the body had disappeared;
not in a grave, of course; but there lay upon him
a little dust as of a hand avoiding
the curse of violating the dead body's sanctity.
There were no signs of any beast nor dog
that came there; he had clearly not been torn.
There was a tide of bad words at one another,
guard taunting guard, and it might well have ended
in blows, for there was no one there to stop it.
Each one of us was the criminal but no one

manifestly so; all denied knowledge of it.   290
We were ready to take hot bars in our hands
or walk through fire, and call on the gods with oaths
that we had neither done it nor were privy
to a plot with anyone, neither in planning
nor yet in execution.
At last when nothing came of all our searching,
there was one man who spoke, made every head
bow to the ground in fear. For we could not
either contradict him nor yet could we see how
if we did what he said we would come out all right.   300
His word was that we must lay information
about this matter to yourself; we could not cover it.
This view prevailed and the lot of the draw chose me,
unlucky me, to win that prize. So here
I am. I did not want to come,
and you don't want to have me. I know that.
For no one likes the messenger of bad news.

CHORUS: My lord: I wonder, could this be God's doing?
This is the thought that keeps on haunting me.

CREON: Stop, before your words fill even me with rage,   310
that you should be exposed as a fool, and you so old.
For what you say is surely insupportable
when you say the gods took forethought for this corpse.
Is it out of excess of honor for the man,
for the favors that he did them, they should cover him?
This man who came to burn their pillared temples,
their dedicated offerings—and this land
and laws he would have scattered to the winds?
Or do you see the gods as honoring
criminals? This is not so. But what I am doing   320
now, and other things before this, some men disliked,
within this very city, and muttered against me,
secretly shaking their heads; they would not bow

justly beneath the yoke to submit to me.
I am very sure that these men hired others
to do this thing. I tell you the worst currency
that ever grew among mankind is money. This
sacks cities, this drives people from their homes,
this teaches and corrupts the minds of the loyal
330   to acts of shame. This displays
all kinds of evil for the use of men,
instructs in the knowledge of every impious act.
Those that have done this deed have been paid to do it,
but in the end they will pay for what they have done.

It is as sure as I still reverence Zeus—
know this right well—and I speak under oath—
if you and your fellows do not find this man
who with his own hand did the burial
and bring him here before me face to face,
340   your death alone will not be enough for me.
You will hang alive till you open up this outrage.
That will teach you in the days to come from what
you may draw profit—safely—from your plundering.
It's not from anything and everything
you can grow rich. You will find out
that ill-gotten gains ruin more than they save.

SENTRY: Have I your leave to say something—or should I
    just turn and go?

CREON: Don't you know your talk is painful enough
    already?

350 SENTRY: Is the ache in your ears or in your mind?

CREON: Why do you dissect the whereabouts of my pain?

SENTRY: Because it is he who did the deed who hurts
    your mind. I only hurt your ears that listen.

CREON: I am sure you have been a chatterbox since
    you were born.

SENTRY: All the same, I did not do this thing.

CREON: You might have done this, too, if you sold your
    soul.

SENTRY: It's a bad thing if one judges and judges wrongly.

CREON: You may talk as wittily as you like of judgment.
    Only, if you don't bring to light those men
    who have done this, you will yet come to say   360
    that your wretched gains have brought bad
    consequences.

SENTRY: (*aside*) It were best that he were found, but
    whether
    the criminal is taken or he isn't—
    for that chance will decide—one thing is certain,
    you'll never see me coming here again.
    I never hoped to escape, never thought I could.
    But now I have come off safe, I thank God heartily.

CHORUS: Many are the wonders, none
        is more wonderful than what is man. / ¹
        This it is that crosses the sea   370
        with the south winds storming and the waves
            swelling,
        breaking around him in roaring surf. / ²
        He it is again who wears away
        the Earth, oldest of gods, immortal, unwearied,
        as the ploughs wind across her from year to year
        when he works her with the breed that comes
            from horses. / ³

        The tribe of the lighthearted birds he snares
        and takes prisoner the races of savage beasts
        and the brood of the fish of the sea,

380   with the close-spun web of nets. / 4
A cunning fellow is man. /His contrivances
make him master of beasts of the field
and those that move in the mountains. / 6
So he brings the horse with the shaggy neck
to bend underneath the yoke; / 7
and also the untamed mountain bull; / 8
and speech and windswift thought
and the tempers that go with city living
he has taught himself, /and how to avoid
390   the sharp frost, when lodging is cold
under the open sky
and pelting strokes of the rain. / 10
He has a way against everything,
and he faces nothing that is to come
without contrivance. / 11
Only against death
can he call on no means of escape; / 12
but escape from hopeless diseases
he has found in the depths of his mind. / 13
400   With some sort of cunning, inventive
beyond all expectation
he reaches sometimes evil,
and sometimes good. / 14

If he honors the laws of earth,
and the justice of the gods he has confirmed by
         oath,
high is his city; /no city
has he with whom dwells dishonor
prompted by recklessness. / 16
He who is so, may he never
410   share my hearth! / 17
may he never think my thoughts! / 18

Is this a portent sent by God? / *19*
I cannot tell. / *20*
I know her / How can I say *21*
that this is not Antigone? / *22* Jamie Matthews
Unhappy girl, child of unhappy Oedipus,
what is this? / *23* Cree
Surely it is not you they bring here
as disobedient to the royal edict, / *24*
surely not you, taken in such folly. / *25* 420

SENTRY: She is the one who did the deed;
we took her burying him. But where is Creon?

CHORUS: He is just coming from the house, when you
most need him.

CREON: What is this? What has happened that I come
so opportunely?

SENTRY: My lord, there is nothing
that a man should swear he would never do.
Second thoughts make liars of the first resolution.
I would have vowed it would be long enough
before I came again, lashed hence by your threats. 430
But since the joy that comes past hope, and against all
hope,
is like no other pleasure in extent,
I have come here, though I break my oath in coming.
I bring this girl here who has been captured
giving the grace of burial to the dead man.
This time no lot chose me; this was my jackpot,
and no one else's. Now, my lord, take her
and as you please judge her and test her; I
am justly free and clear of all this trouble.

CREON: This girl—how did you take her and from where? 440

SENTRY: She was burying the man. Now you know all.

CREON: Do you know what you are saying? Do you
    mean it?

SENTRY: She is the one; I saw her burying
    the dead man you forbade the burial of.
    Now, do I speak plainly and clearly enough?

CREON: How was she seen? How was she caught in
    the act?

SENTRY: This is how it was. When we came there,
    with those dreadful threats of yours upon us,
    we brushed off all the dust that lay upon
450   the dead man's body, heedfully
    leaving it moist and naked.
    We sat on the brow of the hill, to windward,
    that we might shun the smell of the corpse upon us.
    Each of us wakefully urged his fellow
    with torrents of abuse, not to be careless
    in this work of ours. So it went on,
    until in the midst of the sky the sun's bright circle
    stood still; the heat was burning. Suddenly
    a squall lifted out of the earth a storm of dust,
460   a trouble in the sky. It filled the plain,
    ruining all the foliage of the wood
    that was around it. The great empty air
    was filled with it. We closed our eyes, enduring
    this plague sent by the gods. When at long last
    we were quit of it, why, then we saw the girl.

    She was crying out with the shrill cry
    of an embittered bird
    that sees its nest robbed of its nestlings
    and the bed empty. So, too, when she saw
470   the body stripped of its cover, she burst out in groans,
    calling terrible curses on those that had done that deed;

and with her hands immediately
brought thirsty dust to the body; from a shapely brazen
urn, held high over it, poured a triple stream
of funeral offerings; and crowned the corpse.
When we saw that, we rushed upon her and
caught our quarry then and there, not a bit disturbed.
We charged her with what she had done, then and the
   first time.
She did not deny a word of it—to my joy,
but to my pain as well. It is most pleasant   480
to have escaped oneself out of such troubles
but painful to bring into it those whom we love.
However, it is but natural for me
to count all this less than my own escape.

CREON: You there, that turn your eyes upon the ground,
   do you confess or deny what you have done?

ANTIGONE: Yes, I confess; I will not deny my deed.

CREON: (*to the Sentry*) You take yourself off where you like.
   You are free of a heavy charge.
   Now, Antigone, tell me shortly and to the point,   490
   did you know the proclamation against your action?

ANTIGONE: I knew it; of course I did. For it was public.

CREON: And did you dare to disobey that law?

ANTIGONE: Yes, it was not Zeus that made the
      proclamation;
   nor did Justice, which lives with those below, enact
   such laws as that, for mankind. I did not believe
   your proclamation had such power to enable
   one who will someday die to override
   God's ordinances, unwritten and secure.
   They are not of today and yesterday;   500

they live forever; none knows when first they were.
These are the laws whose penalties I would not
incur from the gods, through fear of any man's temper.

I know that I will die—of course I do—
even if you had not doomed me by proclamation.
If I shall die before my time, I count that
a profit. How can such as I, that live
among such troubles, not find a profit in death?
So for such as me, to face such a fate as this
510   is pain that does not count. But if I dared to leave
the dead man, my mother's son, dead and unburied,
that would have been real pain. The other is not.
Now, if you think me a fool to act like this,
perhaps it is a fool that judges so.

CHORUS: The savage spirit of a savage father
shows itself in this girl. She does not know
how to yield to trouble.

CREON: I would have you know the most fanatic spirits
fall most of all. It is the toughest iron,
520   baked in the fire to hardness, you may see
most shattered, twisted, shivered to fragments.
I know hot horses are restrained
by a small curb. For he that is his neighbor's slave
cannot
be high in spirit. This girl had learned her insolence
before this, when she broke the established laws.
But here is still another insolence
in that she boasts of it, laughs at what she did.
I swear I am no man and she the man
if she can win this and not pay for it.
530   No; though she were my sister's child or closer
in blood than all that my hearth god acknowledges
as mine, neither she nor her sister should escape

the utmost sentence—death. For indeed I accuse her,
the sister, equally of plotting the burial.
Summon her. I saw her inside, just now,
crazy, distraught. When people plot
mischief in the dark, it is the mind which first
is convicted of deceit. But surely I hate indeed
the one that is caught in evil and then makes
that evil look like good.   540

ANTIGONE: Do you want anything
beyond my taking and my execution?

CREON: Oh, nothing! Once I have that I have everything.

ANTIGONE: Why do you wait, then? Nothing that you say
pleases me; God forbid it ever should.
So my words, too, naturally offend you.
Yet how could I win a greater share of glory
than putting my own brother in his grave?
All that are here would surely say that's true,
if fear did not lock their tongues up. A prince's power   550
is blessed in many things, not least in this,
that he can say and do whatever he likes.

CREON: You are alone among the people of Thebes
to see things in that way.

ANTIGONE: No, these do, too,
but keep their mouths shut for the fear of you.

CREON: Are you not ashamed to think so differently
from them?

ANTIGONE: There is nothing shameful in honoring my
brother.

CREON: Was not he that died on the other side your
brother?   560

ANTIGONE: Yes, indeed, of my own blood from father and
    mother.

CREON: Why then do you show a grace that must be
        impious
    in *his* sight?

ANTIGONE: *That* other dead man
    would never bear you witness in what you say.

CREON: Yes he would, if you put him only on equality
    with one that was a desecrator.

ANTIGONE: It was his brother, not his slave, that died.

CREON: He died destroying the country the other
        defended.

ANTIGONE: The god of death demands these rites for
570   both.

CREON: But the good man does not seek an *equal* share
        only,
    with the bad.

ANTIGONE: Who knows
    if in that other world this is true piety?

CREON: My enemy is still my enemy, even in death.

ANTIGONE: My nature is to join in love, not hate.

CREON: Go then to the world below, yourself, if you
    must love. Love *them*. When I am alive no woman shall
        rule.

CHORUS: Here before the gates comes Ismene
580   shedding tears for the love of a brother.
    A cloud over her brow casts shame
    on her flushed face, as the tears wet
    her fair cheeks.

CREON: You there, who lurked in my house, viper-like—
  secretly drawing its lifeblood; I never thought
  that I was raising two sources of destruction,
  two rebels against my throne. Come tell me now,
  will you, too, say you bore a hand in the burial
  or will you swear that you know nothing of it?

ISMENE: I did it, yes—if she will say I did it   590
  I bear my share in it, bear the guilt, too.

ANTIGONE: Justice will not allow you what you refused
  and I will have none of your partnership.

ISMENE: But in your troubles I am not ashamed
  to sail with you the sea of suffering.

ANTIGONE: Where the act was death, the dead are
    witnesses.
  I do not love a friend who loves in words.

ISMENE: Sister, do not dishonor me, denying me
  a common death with you, a common honoring
  of the dead man.   600

ANTIGONE: Don't die with me, nor make your own
  what you have never touched. I that die am enough.

ISMENE: What life is there for me, once I have lost you?

ANTIGONE: Ask Creon; all your care was on his behalf.

ISMENE: Why do you hurt me, when you gain nothing by
    it?

ANTIGONE: I am hurt by my own mockery—if I mock
  you.

ISMENE: Even now—what can I do to help you still?

ANTIGONE: Save yourself; I do not grudge you your
  escape.

ISMENE: I cannot bear it! Not even to share your death!

610   ANTIGONE: Life was your choice, and death was mine.

ISMENE: You cannot say I accepted that choice in silence.

ANTIGONE: You were right in the eyes of one party, I in
    the other.

ISMENE: Well then, the fault is equally between us.

ANTIGONE: Take heart; you are alive, but my life died
    long ago, to serve the dead.

CREON: Here are two girls; I think that one of them
    has suddenly lost her wits—the other was always so.

ISMENE: Yes, for, my lord, the wits that they are born with
    do not stay firm for the unfortunate.
620   They go astray.

CREON: Certainly yours do,
    when you share troubles with the troublemaker.

ISMENE: What life can be mine alone without her?

CREON: Do not
    speak of *her*. *She* isn't, anymore.

ISMENE: Will you kill your son's wife to be?

CREON: Yes, there are other fields for him to plough.

ISMENE: Not with the mutual love of him and her.

CREON: I hate a bad wife for a son of mine.

ANTIGONE: Dear Haemon, how your father dishonors
630   you.

CREON: There is too much of you—and of your marriage!

CHORUS: Will you rob your son of this girl?

CREON: Death—it is death that will stop the marriage for
me.

CHORUS: Your decision it seems is taken: she shall die.

CREON: Both you and I have decided it. No more delay.
(*He turns to the servants.*)

Bring her inside, you. From this time forth,
these must be women, and not free to roam.
For even the stout of heart shrink when they see
the approach of death close to their lives.

CHORUS: Lucky are those whose lives   640
know no taste of sorrow.
But for those whose house has been shaken by
God
there is never cessation of ruin;
it steals on generation after generation
within a breed. Even as the swell
is driven over the dark deep
by the fierce Thracian winds
I see the ancient evils of Labdacus' house
are heaped on the evils of the dead.
No generation frees another, some god   650
strikes them down; there is no deliverance.
Here was the light of hope stretched
over the last roots of Oedipus' house,
and the bloody dust due to the gods below
has mowed it down—that and the folly of speech
and ruin's enchantment of the mind.

Your power, O Zeus, what sin of man can limit?
All-aging sleep does not overtake it,
nor the unwearied months of the gods; and you,
for whom time brings no age,   660
you hold the glowing brightness of Olympus.

For the future near and far,
and the past, this law holds good:
nothing very great
comes to the life of mortal man
without ruin to accompany it.
For Hope, widely wandering, comes to many of
 mankind
as a blessing,
but to many as the deceiver,
670 using light-minded lusts;
she comes to him that knows nothing
till he burns his foot in the glowing fire.
With wisdom has someone declared
a word of distinction:
that evil seems good to one whose mind
the god leads to ruin,
and but for the briefest moment of time
is his life outside of calamity.

Here is Haemon, youngest of your sons.
680 Does he come grieving
for the fate of his bride to be,
in agony at being cheated of his marriage?

CREON: Soon we will know that better than the prophets.
My son, can it be that you have not heard
of my final decision on your betrothed?
Can you have come here in your fury against your
 father?
Or have I your love still, no matter what I do?

HAEMON: Father, I am yours; with your excellent
 judgment
you lay the right before me, and I shall follow it.
690 No marriage will ever be so valued by me
as to override the goodness of your leadership.

CREON: Yes, my son, this should always be
   in your very heart, that everything else
   shall be second to your father's decision.
   It is for this that fathers pray to have
   obedient sons begotten in their halls,
   that they may requite with ill their father's enemy
   and honor his friend no less than he would himself.
   If a man have sons that are no use to him,
   what can one say of him but that he has bred   700
   so many sorrows to himself, laughter to his enemies?
   Do not, my son, banish your good sense
   through pleasure in a woman, since you know
   that the embrace grows cold
   when an evil woman shares your bed and home.
   What greater wound can there be than a false friend?
   No. Spit on her, throw her out like an enemy,
   this girl, to marry someone in Death's house.
   I caught her openly in disobedience
   alone out of all this city and I shall not make   710
   myself a liar in the city's sight. No, I will kill her.
   So let her cry if she will on the Zeus of kinship;
   for if I rear those of my race and breeding
   to be rebels, surely I will do so with those outside it.
   For he who is in his household a good man
   will be found a just man, too, in the city.
   But he that breaches the law or does it violence
   or thinks to dictate to those who govern him
   shall never have my good word.
   The man the city sets up in authority   720
   must be obeyed in small things and in just
   but also in their opposites.
   I am confident such a man of whom I speak
   will be a good ruler, and willing to be well ruled.
   He will stand on his country's side, faithful and just,
   in the storm of battle. There is nothing worse

than disobedience to authority.
It destroys cities, it demolishes homes;
it breaks and routs one's allies. Of successful lives
730   the most of them are saved by discipline.
So we must stand on the side of what is orderly;
we cannot give victory to a woman.
If we must accept defeat, let it be from a man;
we must not let people say that a woman beat us.

CHORUS: We think, if we are not victims of Time the
    Thief,
that you speak intelligently of what you speak.

HAEMON: Father, the natural sense that the gods breed
    in men is surely the best of their possessions.
I certainly could not declare you wrong—
740   may I never know how to do so!—Still there might
be something useful that some other than you might
    think.
It is natural for me to be watchful on your behalf
concerning what all men say or do or find to blame.
Your face is terrible to a simple citizen;
it frightens him from words you dislike to hear.
But what *I* can hear, in the dark, are things like these:
the city mourns for this girl; they think she is dying
most wrongly and most undeservedly
of all womenkind, for the most glorious acts.
750   Here is one who would not leave her brother unburied,
a brother who had fallen in bloody conflict,
to meet his end by greedy dogs or by
the bird that chanced that way. Surely what she merits
is golden honor, isn't it? That's the dark rumor
that spreads in secret. Nothing I own
I value more highly, father, than your success.
What greater distinction can a son have than the glory
of a successful father, and for a father

the distinction of successful children?
Do not bear this single habit of mind, to think   760
that what you say and nothing else is true.
A man who thinks that he alone is right,
or what he says, or what he *is* himself,
unique, such men, when opened up, are seen
to be quite empty. For a man, though he be wise,
it is no shame to learn—learn many things,
and not maintain his views too rigidly.
You notice how by streams in wintertime
the trees that yield preserve their branches safely,
but those that fight the tempest perish utterly.   770
The man who keeps the sheet of his sail tight
and never slackens capsizes his boat
and makes the rest of his trip keel uppermost.
Yield something of your anger, give way a little.
If a much younger man, like me, may have
a judgment, I would say it were far better
to be one altogether wise by nature, but,
as things incline not to be so, then it is good
also to learn from those who advise well.

CHORUS: My lord, if he says anything to the point,   780
     you should learn from him, and you, too, Haemon,
     learn from your father. Both of you
     have spoken well.

CREON: Should we that are my age learn wisdom
     from young men such as he is?

HAEMON: Not learn injustice, certainly. If I am young,
     do not look at my years but what I do.

CREON: Is what you do to have respect for rebels?

HAEMON: I
     would not urge you to be scrupulous   790
     towards the wicked.

CREON: Is *she* not tainted by the disease of wickedness?

HAEMON: The entire people of Thebes says no to that.

CREON: Should the city tell me how I am to rule them?

HAEMON: Do you see what a young man's words these are
of yours?

CREON: Must I rule the land by someone else's judgment
rather than my own?

HAEMON: There is no city
possessed by one man only.

800   CREON: Is not the city thought to be the ruler's?

HAEMON: You would be a fine dictator of a desert.

CREON: It seems this boy is on the woman's side.

HAEMON: If you are a woman—my care is all for you.

CREON: You villain, to bandy words with your own
father!

HAEMON: I see your acts as mistaken and unjust.

CREON: Am I mistaken, reverencing my own office?

HAEMON: There is no reverence in trampling on God's
honor.

CREON: Your nature is vile, in yielding to a woman.

HAEMON: You will not find me yield to what is shameful.

810   CREON: At least, your argument is all for her.

HAEMON: Yes, and for you and me—and for the gods
below.

CREON: You will never marry her while her life lasts.

HAEMON: Then she must die—and dying destroy another.

CREON: Has your daring gone so far, to threaten me?

HAEMON: What threat is it to speak against empty
     judgments?

CREON: Empty of sense yourself, you will regret
     your schooling of me in sense.

HAEMON: If you were not
     my father, I would say you are insane.

CREON: You woman's slave, do not try to wheedle me.   820

HAEMON: You want to talk but never to hear and listen.

CREON: Is that so? By the heavens above you will not—
     be sure of that—get off scot-free, insulting,
     abusing me.
(*He speaks to the servants.*)

                    You people bring out this creature,
     this hated creature, that she may die before
     his very eyes, right now, next her would-be husband.

HAEMON: Not at my side! Never think that! She will not
     die by my side. But you will never again
     set eyes upon my face. Go then and rage   830
     with such of your friends as are willing to endure it.

CHORUS: The man is gone, my lord, quick in his anger.
     A young man's mind is fierce when he is hurt.

CREON: Let him go, and do and think things superhuman.
     But these two girls he shall not save from death.

CHORUS: Both of them? Do you mean to kill them both?

CREON: No, not the one that didn't do anything.
     You are quite right there.

CHORUS: And by what form of death do you mean to
kill her?

840   CREON: I will bring her where the path is loneliest,
and hide her alive in a rocky cavern there.
I'll give just enough of food as shall suffice
for a bare expiation, that the city may avoid pollution.
In that place she shall call on Hades, god of death,
in her prayers. That god only she reveres.
Perhaps she will win from him escape from death
or at least in that last moment will recognize
her honoring of the dead is labor lost.

CHORUS: Love undefeated in the fight,
850   Love that makes havoc of possessions,
Love who lies at night in a young girl's soft
cheeks,
Who travels over sea, or in huts in the
countryside—
there is no god able to escape you
nor anyone of men, whose life is a day only,
and whom you possess is mad.

You wrench the minds of just men to injustice,
to their disgrace; this conflict among kinsmen
it is you who stirred to turmoil.
The winner is desire. She gleaming kindles
860   from the eyes of the girl good to bed.
Loves shares the throne with the great powers
that rule.
For the golden Aphrodite holds her play there
and then no one can overcome her.

Here I too am borne out of the course of
lawfulness
when I see these things, and I cannot control
the springs of my tears
when I see Antigone making her way
to her bed—but the bed
that is rest for everyone.

ANTIGONE: You see me, you people of my country,   870
    as I set out on my last road of all,
    looking for the last time on this light of this sun—
    never again. I am alive but Hades who gives sleep to
        everyone
    is leading me to the shores of Acheron,
    though I have known nothing of marriage songs
    nor the chant that brings the bride to bed.
    My husband is to be the Lord of Death.

CHORUS: Yes, you go to the place where the dead are
        hidden,
    but you go with distinction and praise.
    You have not been stricken by wasting sickness;   880
    you have not earned the wages of the sword;
    it was your own choice and alone among mankind
    you will descend, alive,
    to that world of death.

ANTIGONE: But indeed I have heard of the saddest of
        deaths—
    of the Phrygian stranger, daughter of Tantalus,
    whom the rocky growth subdued, like clinging ivy.
    The rains never leave her, the snow never fails,
    as she wastes away. That is how men tell the story.
    From streaming eyes her tears wet the crags;   890
    most like to her the god brings me to rest.

CHORUS: Yes, but she was a god, and god born,
    and you are mortal and mortal born.
    Surely it is great renown
    for a woman that dies, that in life and death
    her lot is a lot shared with demigods.

ANTIGONE: You mock me. In the name of our fathers'
    gods

why do you not wait till I am gone to insult me?
Must you do it face to face?
900   My city! Rich citizens of my city!
You springs of Dirce, you holy groves of Thebes,
famed for its chariots! I would still have you as my
    witnesses,
with what dry-eyed friends, under what laws
I make my way to my prison sealed like a tomb.
Pity me. Neither among the living nor the dead
do I have a home in common—
neither with the living nor the dead.

CHORUS: You went to the extreme of daring
and against the high throne of Justice
910   you fell, my daughter, grievously.
But perhaps it was for some ordeal of your father
that you are paying requital.

ANTIGONE: You have touched the most painful of my
    cares—
the pity for my father, ever reawakened,
and the fate of all of our race, the famous Labdacids;
the doomed self-destruction of my mother's bed
when she slept with her own son,
my father.
What parents I was born of, God help me!
920   To them I am going to share their home,
the curse on me, too, and unmarried.
Brother, it was a luckless marriage you made,
and dying killed my life.

CHORUS: There *is* a certain reverence for piety.
But for him in authority,
he cannot see that authority defied;
it is your own self-willed temper
that has destroyed you.

ANTIGONE: No tears for me, no friends, no marriage.
    Brokenhearted
  I am led along the road ready before me.   930
  I shall never again be suffered
  to look on the holy eye of the day.
  But my fate claims no tears—
  no friend cries for me.

CREON: (*to the servants*) Don't you know that weeping and
    wailing before death
  would never stop if one is allowed to weep and wail?
  Lead away at once. Enfold her
  in that rocky tomb of hers—as I told you to.
  There leave her alone, solitary,
  to die if she so wishes   940
  or live a buried life in such a home;
  we are guiltless in respect of her, this girl.
  But living above, among the rest of us, this life
  she shall certainly lose.

ANTIGONE: Tomb, bridal chamber, prison forever
  dug in rock, it is to you I am going
  to join my people, that great number that have died,
  whom in their death Persephone received.
  I am the last of them and I go down
  in the worst death of all—for I have not lived   950
  the due term of my life. But when I come
  to that other world my hope is strong
  that my coming will be welcome to my father,
  and dear to you, my mother, and dear to you,
  my brother deeply loved. For when you died,
  with my own hands I washed and dressed you all,
  and poured the lustral offerings on your graves.
  And now, Polyneices, it was for such care of your body
  that I have earned these wages.
  Yet those who think rightly will think I did right   960

in honoring you. Had I been a mother
of children, and my husband been dead and rotten,
I would not have taken this weary task upon me
against the will of the city. What law backs me
when I say this? I will tell you:
If my husband were dead, I might have had another,
and child from another man, if I lost the first.
But when father and mother both were hidden in death
no brother's life would bloom for me again.

970 That is the law under which I gave you precedence,
my dearest brother, and that is why Creon thinks me
wrong, even a criminal, and now takes me
by the hand and leads me away,
unbedded, without bridal, without share
in marriage and in nurturing of children;
as lonely as you see me; without friends;
with fate against me I go to the vault of death
while still alive. What law of God have I broken?
Why should I still look to the gods in my misery?

980 Whom should I summon as ally? For indeed
because of piety I was called impious.
If this proceeding is good in the gods' eyes
I shall know my sin, once I have suffered.
But if Creon and his people are the wrongdoers
let their suffering be no worse than the injustice
they are meting out to me.

CHORUS: It is the same blasts, the tempests of the soul,
    possess her.

CREON: Then for this her guards,
990   who are so slow, will find themselves in trouble.

ANTIGONE: (*cries out*) Oh, that word has come
    very close to death.

CREON: I will not comfort you
    with hope that the sentence will not be accomplished.

ANTIGONE: O my father's city, in Theban land,
  O gods that sired my race,
  I am led away, I have no more stay.
  Look on me, princes of Thebes,
  the last remnant of the old royal line;
  see what I suffer and who makes me suffer   1000
  because I gave reverence to what claims reverence.

CHORUS: Danae suffered, too, when, her beauty lost, she
          gave
        the light of heaven in exchange for brassbound
          walls,
        and in the tomb-like cell was she hidden and
          held;
        yet she was honored in her breeding, child,
        and she kept, as guardian, the seed of Zeus
        that came to her in a golden shower.
        But there is some terrible power in destiny
        and neither wealth nor war
        nor tower nor black ships, beaten by the sea,   1010
        can give escape from it.

        The hot-tempered son of Dryas, the Edonian
          king,
        in fury mocked Dionysus,
        who then held him in restraint
        in a rocky dungeon.
        So the terrible force and flower of his madness
        drained away. He came to know the god
        whom in frenzy he had touched with his
          mocking tongue,
        when he would have checked the inspired
          women
        and the fire of Dionysus,   1020
        when he provoked the Muses that love the lyre.
        By the black rocks, dividing the sea in two,
        are the shores of the Bosporus, Thracian
          Salmydessus.

There the god of war who lives near the city
saw the terrible blinding wound
dealt by his savage wife
on Phineus' two sons.
She blinded and tore with the points of her
    shuttle,
and her bloodied hands, those eyes
1030   that else would have looked on her vengefully.
As they wasted away, they lamented
their unhappy fate that they were doomed
to be born of a mother cursed in her marriage.
She traced her descent from the seed
of the ancient Erechtheidae.
In far-distant caves she was raised
among her father's storms, that child of Boreas,
quick as a horse, over the steep hills,
a daughter of the gods.
1040   But, my child, the long-lived Fates
bore hard upon her, too.

(*Enter Teiresias, the blind prophet, led by a boy.*)

TEIRESIAS: My lords of Thebes, we have come here
    together,
    one pair of eyes serving us both. For the blind
    such must be the way of going, by a guide's leading.

CREON: What is the news, my old Teiresias?

TEIRESIAS: I will tell you; and you, listen to the prophet.

CREON: Never in the past have I turned from your advice.

TEIRESIAS: And so you have steered well the ship of state.

CREON: I have benefited and can testify to that.

1050   TEIRESIAS: Then realize you are on the razor edge
    of danger.

CREON: What can that be? I shudder to hear those words.

TEIRESIAS: When you learn the signs recognized by my art
you will understand.
I sat at my ancient place of divination
for watching the birds, where every bird finds shelter;
and I heard an unwonted voice among them;
they were horribly distressed, and screamed
unmeaningly.
I knew they were tearing each other murderously;
the beating of their wings was a clear sign.   1060
I was full of fear; at once on all the altars,
as they were fully kindled, I tasted the offerings,
but the god of fire refused to burn from the sacrifice,
and from the thighbones a dark stream of moisture
oozed from the embers, smoked and sputtered.
The gall bladder burst and scattered to the air
and the streaming thighbones lay exposed
from the fat wrapped round them—
so much I learned from this boy here,
the fading prophecies of a rite that failed.   1070
This boy here is my guide, as I am others'.
This is the city's sickness—and your plans are the
cause of it.
For our altars and our sacrificial hearths
are filled with the carrion meat of birds and dogs,
torn from the flesh of Oedipus' poor son.
So the gods will not take our prayers or sacrifice
nor yet the flame from the thighbones, and no bird
cries shrill and clear, so glutted
are they with fat of the blood of the killed man.
Reflect on these things, son. All men   1080
can make mistakes; but, once mistaken,
a man is no longer stupid nor accursed
who, having fallen on ill, tries to cure that ill,

not taking a fine undeviating stand.
It is obstinacy that convicts of folly.
Yield to the dead man; do not stab him—
now he is gone—what bravery is this,
to inflict another death upon the dead?
I mean you well and speak well for your good.
1090   It is never sweeter to learn from a good counselor
than when he counsels to your benefit.

CREON: Old man, you are all archers, and I am your mark.
I must be tried by your prophecies as well.
By the breed of you I have been bought and sold
and made a merchandise, for ages now.
But I tell you: make your profit from silver-gold
from Sardis and the gold from India
if you will. But this dead man you shall not hide
in a grave, not though the eagles of Zeus should bear
1100   the carrion, snatching it to the throne of Zeus itself.
Even so, I shall not so tremble at the pollution
to let you bury him.

                No, I am certain
no human has the power to pollute the gods.
They fall, you old Teiresias, those men,
—so very clever—in a bad fall whenever
they eloquently speak vile words for profit.

TEIRESIAS: I wonder if there's a man who dares
        consider—

CREON: What do you mean? What sort of generalization
1110   is this talk of yours?

TEIRESIAS: How much the best of possessions is the
        ability
    to listen to wise advice?

CREON: As I should imagine that the worst
   injury must be native stupidity.

TEIRESIAS: Now that is exactly where your mind is sick.

CREON: I do not like to answer a seer with insults.

TEIRESIAS: But you do, when you say my prophecies are
   lies.

CREON: Well,
   the whole breed of prophets certainly loves money.

TEIRESIAS: And the breed that comes from princes loves
      to take
   advantage—base advantage.   1120

CREON: Do you realize
   you are speaking in such terms of your own prince?

TEIRESIAS: I know. But it is through me you have saved
      the city.

CREON: You are a wise prophet, but what you love is
      wrong.

TEIRESIAS: You will force me to declare what should be
      hidden
   in my own heart.

CREON: Out with it—
   but only if your words are not for gain.

TEIRESIAS: They won't be for *your* gain—that I am sure of.

CREON: But realize you will not make a merchandise   1130
   of my decisions.

TEIRESIAS: And you must realize
   that you will not outlive many cycles more
   of this swift sun before you give in exchange

one of your own loins bred, a corpse for a corpse,
for you have thrust one that belongs above
below the earth, and bitterly dishonored
a living soul by lodging her in the grave;
while one that belonged indeed to the underworld
1140   gods you have kept on this earth without due share
of rites of burial, of due funeral offerings,
a corpse unhallowed. With all of this you, Creon,
have nothing to do, nor have the gods above.
These acts of yours are violence, on your part.
And in requital the avenging Spirits
of Death itself and the gods' Furies shall
after *your* deeds, lie in ambush for you, and
in their hands you shall be taken cruelly.
Now, look at this and tell me I was bribed
1150   to say it! The delay will not be long
before the cries of mourning in your house,
of men and women. All the cities will stir in hatred
against you, because their sons in mangled shreds
received their burial rites from dogs, from wild beasts
or when some bird of the air brought a vile stink
to each city that contained the hearths of the dead.
These are the arrows that archer-like I launched—
you vexed me so to anger—at your heart.
You shall not escape their sting. You, boy,
1160   lead me away to my house, so he may discharge
his anger on younger men; so may he come to know
to bear a quieter tongue in his head and a better
mind than that now he carries in him.

CHORUS: That was a terrible prophecy, my lord.
The man has gone. Since these hairs of mine grew white
from the black they once were, he has never spoken
a word of a lie to our city.

CREON: I know, I know.
My mind is all bewildered. To yield is terrible.
But by opposition to destroy my very being
with a self-destructive curse must also be reckoned   1170
in what is terrible.

CHORUS: You need good counsel, son of Menoeceus,
and need to take it.

CREON: What must I do, then? Tell me; I shall agree.

CHORUS: The girl—go now and bring her up from her
cave,
and for the exposed dead man, give him his burial.

CREON: That is really your advice? You would have me
yield.

CHORUS: And quickly as you may, my lord. Swift harms
sent by the gods cut off the paths of the foolish.

CREON: Oh, it is hard; I must give up what my heart   1180
would have me do. But it is ill to fight
against what must be.

CHORUS: Go now, and do this;
do not give the task to others.

CREON: I will go,
just as I am. Come, servants, all of you;
take axes in your hands; away with you
to the place you see, there.
For my part, since my intention is so changed,
as I bound her myself, myself will free her.   1190
I am afraid it may be best, in the end
of life, to have kept the old accepted laws.

CHORUS: You of many names, glory of the Cadmeian
bride, breed of loud thundering Zeus;

you who watch over famous Italy;
you who rule where all are welcome in Eleusis;
in the sheltered plains of Deo—
O Bacchus that dwells in Thebes,
the mother city of Bacchanals,
1200   by the flowing stream of Ismenus,
in the ground sown by the fierce dragon's teeth.

You are he on whom the murky gleam of torches
        glares,
above the twin peaks of the crag
where come the Corycean nymphs
to worship you, the Bacchanals;
and the stream of Castalia has seen you, too;
and you are he that the ivy-clad
slopes of Nisaean hills,
and the green shore ivy-clustered,
1210   sent to watch over the roads of Thebes,
where the immortal Evoe chant rings out.

It is Thebes which you honor most of all cities,
you and your mother both,
she who died by the blast of Zeus' thunderbolt.
And now when the city, with all its folk,
is gripped by a violent plague,
come with healing foot, over the slopes of
        Parnassus,
over the moaning strait.
You lead the dance of the fire-breathing stars,
1220   you are master of the voices of the night.
True-born child of Zeus, appear,
my lord, with your Thyiad attendants,
who in frenzy all night long
dance in your house, Iacchus,
dispenser of gifts.

MESSENGER: You who live by the house of Cadmus and
        Amphion,

hear me. There is no condition of man's life
that stands secure. As such I would not
praise it or blame. It is chance that sets upright;
it is chance that brings down the lucky and the unlucky,   1230
each in his turn. For men, that belong to death,
there is no prophet of established things.
Once Creon was a man worthy of envy—
of my envy, at least. For he saved this city
of Thebes from her enemies, and attained
the throne of the land, with all a king's power.
He guided it right. His race bloomed
with good children. But when a man forfeits joy
I do not count his life as life, but only
a life trapped in a corpse.   1240
Be rich within your house, yes greatly rich,
if so you will, and live in a prince's style.
If the gladness of these things is gone, I would not
give the shadow of smoke for the rest,
as against joy.

CHORUS: What is the sorrow of our princes
of which you are the messenger?

MESSENGER: Death; and the living are guilty of their
deaths.

CHORUS: But who is the murderer? Who the murdered?
Tell us.

MESSENGER: Haemon is dead; the hand that shed his
blood   1250
was his very own.

CHORUS: Truly his own hand? Or his father's?

MESSENGER: His own hand, in his anger
against his father for a murder.

CHORUS: Prophet, how truly you have made good your
    word!

MESSENGER: These things are so; you may debate the rest.
    Here I see Creon's wife Eurydice
    approaching. Unhappy woman!
    Does she come from the house as hearing about her son
1260   or has she come by chance?

EURYDICE: I heard your words, all you men of Thebes,
        as I
    was going out to greet Pallas with my prayers.
    I was just drawing back the bolts of the gate
    to open it when a cry struck through my ears
    telling of my household's ruin. I fell backward
    in terror into the arms of my servants; I fainted.
    But tell me again, what is the story? I
    will hear it as one who is no stranger to sorrow.

MESSENGER: Dear mistress, I will tell you, for I was there,
1270   and I will leave out no word of the truth.
    Why should I comfort you and then tomorrow
    be proved a liar? The truth is always best.

    I followed your husband, at his heels, to the end of the
        plain
    where Polyneices' body still lay unpitied,
    and torn by dogs. We prayed to Hecate, goddess
    of the crossroads, and also to Pluto
    that they might restrain their anger and turn kind.
    And him we washed with sacred lustral water
    and with fresh-cut boughs we burned what was left of
        him
1280   and raised a high mound of his native earth;
    then we set out again for the hollowed rock,
    death's stone bridal chamber for the girl.
    Someone then heard a voice of bitter weeping
    while we were still far off, coming from that unblest
        room.

The man came to tell our master Creon of it.
As the king drew nearer, there swarmed about him
a cry of misery but no clear words.
He groaned and in an anguished mourning voice
cried "Oh, am I a true prophet? Is this the road
that I must travel, saddest of all my wayfaring?   1290
It is my son's voice that haunts my ear. Servants,
get closer, quickly. Stand around the tomb
and look. There is a gap there where the stones
have been wrenched away; enter there, by the very
     mouth,
and see whether I recognize the voice of Haemon
or if the gods deceive me." On the command
of our despairing master we went to look.
In the furthest part of the tomb we saw her, hanging
by her neck. She had tied a noose of muslin on it.
Haemon's hands were about her waist embracing her,   1300
while he cried for the loss of his bride gone to the dead,
and for all his father had done, and his own sad love.
When Creon saw him he gave a bitter cry,
went in and called to him with a groan: "Poor son!
what have you done? What can you have meant?
What happened to destroy you? Come out, I pray you!"
The boy glared at him with savage eyes, and then
spat in his face, without a word of answer.
He drew his double-hilted sword. As his father
ran to escape him, Haemon failed to strike him,   1310
and the poor wretch in anger at himself
leaned on his sword and drove it halfway in,
into his ribs. Then he folded the girl to him,
in his arms, while he was conscious still,
and gasping poured a sharp stream of bloody drops
on her white cheeks. There they lie,
the dead upon the dead. So he has won
the pitiful fulfillment of his marriage

within death's house. In this human world he has shown
1320   how the wrong choice in plans is for a man
his greatest evil.

CHORUS: What do you make of this? My lady is gone,
without a word of good or bad.

MESSENGER: I, too,
am lost in wonder. I am inclined to hope
that hearing of her son's death she could not
open her sorrow to the city, but chose rather
within her house to lay upon her maids
the mourning for the household grief. Her judgment
1330   is good; she will not make any false step.

CHORUS: I do not know. To me this over-heavy silence
seems just as dangerous as much empty wailing.

MESSENGER: I will go in and learn if in her passionate
heart she keeps hidden some secret purpose.
You are right; there is sometimes danger in too much
silence.

CHORUS: Here comes our king himself. He bears in his
hands
a memorial all too clear;
it is a ruin of none other's making,
purely his own if one dare to say that.

1340   CREON: The mistakes of a blinded man
are themselves rigid and laden with death.
You look at us the killer and the killed
of the one blood. Oh, the awful blindness
of those plans of mine. My son, you were so young,
so young to die. You were freed from the bonds of life
through no folly of your own—only through mine.

CHORUS: I think you have learned justice—but too late.

CREON: Yes, I have learned it to my bitterness.
    At this moment
  God has sprung on my head with a vast weight
  and struck me down. He shook me in my savage ways;   1350
  he has overturned my joy, has trampled it,
  underfoot. The pains men suffer
  are pains indeed.

SECOND MESSENGER: My lord, you have troubles and a
    store besides;
  some are there in your hands, but there are others
  you will surely see when you come to your house.

CREON: What trouble can there be beside these troubles?

SECOND MESSENGER: The queen is dead. She was indeed
    true mother
  of the dead son. She died, poor lady,
  by recent violence upon herself.   1360

CREON: Haven of death, you can never have enough.
  Why, why do you destroy me?
  You messenger, who have brought me bitter news,
  what is this tale you tell?
  It is a dead man that you kill again—
  what new message of yours is this, boy?
  Is this new slaughter of a woman
  a doom to lie on the pile of the dead?

CHORUS: You can see. It is no longer
  hidden in a corner.   1370

(*By some stage device, perhaps the so-called eccyclema, the inside of
the palace is shown, with the body of the dead Queen.*)

CREON: Here is yet another horror
  for my unhappy eyes to see.
  What doom still waits for me?

I have but now taken in my arms my son,
and again I look upon another dead face.
Poor mother and poor son!

SECOND MESSENGER: She stood at the altar, and with keen
    whetted knife
she suffered her darkening eyes to close.
First she cried in agony recalling the noble fate of
    Megareus,
1380   who died before all this,
and then for the fate of this son; and in the end
she cursed you for the evil you had done
in killing her sons.

CREON: I am distracted with fear. Why does not someone
    strike a two-edged sword right through me?
I am dissolved in an agony of misery.

SECOND MESSENGER: You were indeed accused
    by her that is dead
of Haemon's and of Megareus' death.

1390 CREON: By what kind of violence did she find her
    end?

SECOND MESSENGER: Her own hand struck her to the
    entrails
when she heard of her son's lamentable death.

CREON: These acts can never be made to fit another
to free me from the guilt. It was I that killed her.
Poor wretch that I am, I say it is true!
Servants, lead me away, quickly, quickly.
I am no more a live man than one dead.

CHORUS: What you say is for the best—if there be a best
in evil such as this. For the shortest way
1400   is best with troubles that lie at our feet.

CREON: O, let it come, let it come,
    that best of fates that waits on my last day.
    Surely best fate of all. Let it come, let it come!
    That I may never see one more day's light!

CHORUS: These things are for the future. We must deal
    with what impends. What in the future is to care for
    rests with those whose duty it is
    to care for them.

CREON: At least, all that *I* want
    is in that prayer of mine. 1410

CHORUS: Pray for no more at all. From what is destined
    for us, men mortal, there is no escape.

CREON: Lead me away, a vain silly man
    who killed you, son, and you, too, lady.
    I did not mean to, but I did.
    I do not know where to turn my eyes
    to look to, for support.
    Everything in my hands is crossed. A most unwelcome
      fate
    has leaped upon me.

CHORUS: Wisdom is far the chief element in happiness 1420
    and, secondly, no irreverence towards the gods.
    But great words of haughty men exact
    in retribution blows as great
    and in old age teach wisdom.

NOTES

OEDIPUS THE KING

1 The first word of the play obliquely points to the theme of self-discovery. *Cadmus* is the founder of Thebes.

8 *Great* means 'famous'; cf. 40 ff. and the same word at 1207 (the chorus speaks of Oedipus).

15 *Altar*: at 919 Jocasta turns to an altar at the door (on the stage). Here the altar may be in the center of the orchestra.

22 *Pallas* is a common name for Athena. *Ismenus* refers us to a cult of the local river. *Oracles by fire* are had from examining the remains of sacrificial offerings (see *Antigone* 1006–11).

28 *A God that carries fire*: of the fever; cf. 191. Athens had recently experienced a terrible plague. In *Iliad* I a plague is the means by which Apollo avenges his priest and devastates the Achaean army.

37 *Sphinx*: this monstrous hybrid (commonly represented as a winged lion with the head of a woman) preyed on Thebes until Oedipus solved her riddle; cf. 130, 391, 508, and 1201.

77 *Commands* = 'makes clear'; the appearance of Creon makes his vow a happy omen. Throughout the play Oedipus is represented as a good king blessed by the gods and ready to do their bidding. Cf. 135 f. and 145 f.

97 *King Phoebus* is Apollo; see 151 ff.

123 Note the plural *robbers*; by a common poetic idiom (singular for plural) Oedipus regularly uses the singular, as at 140. The Greek audience knew this ancient story.

151 The *parados* (entrance song) takes the form of a prayer. *Strophe* and *antistrophe* refer to the responsive lyrics.

151–8 *Pytho* is a name for Apollo's shrine at Delphi (cf. 71). *Delian Healer* comes from the god's birthplace (Delos) and a common attribute (he is Paean, the healer, as at 186).

159–67 *Athene* may also be invoked at 188, unless 'deliverance' is personified there. *Far Shooter*: of the archer god Apollo. *Averters of Fate*, i.e., who can ward off death.

177 The *Western God* is Hades, lord of the dead.

190 The *War God* is Ares, whose name begins the Greek stanza. The goddess *Amphitrite* is the consort of Poseidon and here, in opposition to the Black Sea (*Thracian*), probably represents the oceans of the far west.

205 *Lycean* is yet another epithet for Apollo, sometimes etymologically connected with 'light', which jars somewhat with the geographical allusion in *Lycean hills*. Finally, Dionysus (Bacchus), whose mother Semele was Theban, is invoked: *turban of gold* looks to his oriental dress, *Evian* to a shout uttered by his *Maenad* worshippers.

216–75 Public denunciation was the first formal step in Athenian prosecution for murder. It was possible to bring a charge against an unknown criminal, which step was followed by an inquiry into the legitimacy of the charges. Here we find Sophocles utilizing a variety of legal and forensic elements, as well as religious usage (for the curse see 246 and 269), which treat the culprit both as criminal and as one polluting the entire city. An oath (250–51; 276) was required of both parties and was considered strong evidence of guilt and innocence.

242 More than a murderer, the criminal has physically corrupted the city, polluted it, for which Oedipus now forbids him all social and religious converse with it. So *water for his hands* refers to ritual cleansing prior to sacrifice. At a fundamental level this pollution was as physical as the blood shed; consequently, it could contaminate as an evil virus might, and could be driven out and purged, as blood may be washed away.

246 The *curse* is efficacious in religion and in drama. See 269–72, 295, and the allusion to this passage at 1291 and *OC* 865–70.

252 *Fortune* is personified, as if it were an evil demon (cf. 1301 and 1312).

266–8 The Phoenician king *Agenor* sent his sons in search of his lost daughter Europa; one of those sons, *Cadmus*, founded Thebes. The Theban house is often called the Labdacids, after Oedipus' grandfather (cf. 1226).

276 Though designated *Chorus* in this translation, lines in the dialogue (*stichomythia*) are uttered by the choral leader alone.

284 The blind seer *Teiresias* belongs to the Theban tradition. He first

appears in Greek literature in *Odyssey* XI, and offers a dramatically crucial reading of the omens in the *Antigone*.

353 Although Teiresias' accusations become increasingly explicit, they are lost on Oedipus. The king is certain of his innocence and is dealing with an honored seer who refuses to help his city, while claiming to know the 'truth'. Rather naturally the king is outraged, sees a plot (348), and finds more obfuscation and insult (*pollution*) than sense in this passage, where much in the Greek displays an ambiguity that enables Oedipus to find it merely insult. For example, lines 367–8 refer to the king's shameful cohabitation with the dead man's wife, but Oedipus can reasonably hear them as only a charge of shameful association with his friends.

376–7 Most modern editors accept the emendation that underlies this translation. Bollack and Knox dissent, and the latter translates the manuscript: 'It is not destiny that I should fall at your hands, since Apollo is enough, and it is his affair' (*Oedipus at Thebes*, pp. 7–8). The problem turns on the ascription of Oedipus' fate to Apollo, for which only one other passage offers direct testimony (see on 1329a). Whichever reading is accepted, it is well to remember that Teiresias' claim need not mean that Apollo *made* Oedipus do anything. If we accept the emendation, it should be noted that the chorus does not accept the charges as infallibly true (see 496–512).

411 *Loxias* is another name for Apollo; (cf. 853).

418 This *curse*, perhaps personified, is not the same pronounced by Oedipus at 246.

421 The baby Oedipus was exposed on Mount *Cithaeron*; cf. 1090 ff.

437 Oedipus fled from Corinth to protect himself and his parents, and elsewhere in the play he assumes that he knows his parents and that they are Merope and Polybus of Corinth.

442 Several editors accept an emendation that would give us 'skill' for *luck*.

448–61 When does Oedipus exit? If he stays in place, patiently hearing Teiresias out, he would seem to give the old man the final, violent word. Nothing in his subsequent speech suggests he has heard, or understood, this pronouncement. Some readers, however, have objected to such a speech being wasted on a vacated stage. I would take him off at 448.

462–512 In the first stasimon two stanzas are devoted to a meditation on the fate of the murderer, the second pair to the quarrel between Oedipus and Teiresias. Unlike some modern readers, the chorus has not found Teiresias' charges so evidential and compelling that it must condemn the king.

463 *Delphi* is on a mountainside two thousand feet above sea level. Above the actual sanctuary towers Mount *Parnassus* (474).

491 *Labdacus*: see 266–8; *Polybus*: see 437.

545 *Quick ... slow*: very sarcastic; Creon has his turn (549 f.). Cf. 'prophetic mumbler' at 556.

568 From the *Iliad* to Plato there is sufficient distrust, and outright rejection, of seers and prophets to make Oedipus' skepticism familiar and intelligible to the audience. Jocasta will take a similar line (707 ff.). Aristophanes and Plato lead us to believe there were more than a few augural quacks on the streets. The audience also knows, however, that in stories these mediators between the divine and human seldom err.

583 Creon's extensive defense is elaborated from arguments of probability and challenges for proof. Similarly forensic speeches are common in later tragedy; this one shows only the tenacious prejudice of Oedipus.

626–9 The four lines in the Greek are in *antilabe* (a line divided between two or more speakers). Interrupted sentence, abuse, and exclamation reflect their anger.

634 Having reached an impasse, they are extricated by the queen, whose attempt to still the troubled waters will accidentally bring the investigation to a new stage.

644–6 Here Creon takes the oath (see 648 and 653) that he is not guilty as charged. At 656 the chorus also alludes to the powerful oath (*before all men's eyes* seems to be a misreading of the Greek).

649–96 With the exception 669–78, this passage is in lyric meters and was sung.

658–9 He reasons that if he accepts the oath and so dismisses the conspiracy, he must answer to Teiresias' charges (362) and suffer his own curse (*death or banishment*).

705–25 In that both can point to a case in which prophets seem to have failed, Jocasta's skepticism is of a piece with her husband's. He pointed to Teiresias' failure to save the city from the Sphinx; she adduces the Delphic pronouncement that Laius would be killed by his own son. She blames priests (*his servants*), not the god. Earlier versions of this prophecy simply interdicted getting a child, on pain of death. *Where three roads meet*: this is the phrase that alarms Oedipus (see 730). Exposure of infants is a common motif in ancient myth, as well as an historical phenomenon. The *pierced ankles* give him his significant name ('Swellfoot'); such binding would lessen still further his chances of survival. But the baby is turned over to the *hands of others* so that the family itself will not be directly implicated in the death of its own. *Failed* (721) and *false* (723) should not be taken as blasphemy; she simply means that the god did not accomplish the oracles. She is not impious and a little later will pray to Apollo (911–23).

771   Jocasta knows his origin in Corinth, but Oedipus has never told his wife the secret fear that inspired his flight. This speech, while largely a narrative of past events until line 813, reveals both to her and to the audience circumstances of a personal nature.

776   He was *greatest of the citizens* because he was heir apparent.

789   He asked 'Who are my parents?' but the oracle's (*Phoebus* = Apollo) response addressed his fate rather than his parentage (so *unhonored*). To avoid that fate he fled toward Thebes, away from Corinth (794b–798). Both Laius and Oedipus consult Apollo; both attempt to escape the prediction. In Greek myth Catreus learns from an oracle that his son will kill him, Acrisius that his daughter's child will kill him. Both oracles are eventually realized, despite the best efforts of father and grandfather to avoid them. Through negligence Theseus is implicated in the death of his father.

812–22   Greek myth is violent business. Oedipus does not repent these killings, and an Athenian court might well have acquitted him on grounds of self-defense. His only concern, for the moment, is that, if he has killed the previous king and taken his wife, he is the pollution on the city. *Hated by the Gods* means 'has a hostile daimon' (similarly 829), a more personal way of seeing the matter, which brings it close to the theme of chance (774a, 777).

863–910   This second stasimon has raised as much critical controversy as any passage in Sophocles. More detailed notes should be consulted on questions of allusion, diction, ambiguity, and thematic continuities.

863–71   It is not so obvious how these lines continue, or respond to, the previous scene. Most critics seem to think their piety is a reaction to Jocasta's skepticism. *Destiny*: perhaps, 'may my lot/ way ever be ...' *Prescribed*: the *laws* (*nomoi*) comprise the totality of religious and social belief that we call 'culture', but this passage ascribes to them an immutable character untouched by mortality and human negligence. *Olympus* is the home of the gods, and a mountain in Thessaly; the common equation with sky/heaven does not seem apt here (after *clear air of heaven*). It is customary to accept with reverence the Delphic oracles, even when their meaning is unclear or they seem not to predict truly.

872–82 If the previous strophe refers, obliquely, to Jocasta, these lines should refer to Oedipus. *Tyrant* is common in tragedy for 'king' and is so used at 1094a. Have we seen *insolence* (*hybris*) in his treatment of Creon? The imagery of overweening ascent followed by precipitate fall hardly squares with their affectionate concern and regard for Oedipus, which may be alluded to in 880–82. Whether or not they consciously refer to Oedipus, *feet* must call him to mind. *No service* seems a latent metaphor from the road of life and stumbling.

883–96 The second strophe seems to elaborate on themes from the last stanza. If the chorus thinks of the killer of Laius, then its description of him is very abstract. Oedipus cannot be said to *give no heed to Justice*. *Dance* naturally points to their present activity, what the chorus does to honor the god and play its part in the drama; it is also a function of many religious celebrations.

897–910 If oracular utterance is not valid, then there is no reason to travel to *Abae* (an oracle of Apollo in Phocis), or Delphi, or *Olympia* (center of the worship of Zeus). In its enthusiastic piety the chorus prays to Zeus to take a hand in the matter – but if they find it answered, Oedipus is in worse trouble than he suspects.

911 No atheist, Jocasta supplicates Apollo (there is an altar near the door, as was common for Greek houses) for a resolution of their problems. No sooner has she prayed than the answer comes from Corinth.

964 The words translated *Ha! Ha!* are not usually triumphant, but 970–72 certainly seem so. He has not forgotten his fear (974), and relief may be more the tone here.

977 The Sophists made *chance* and nature first 'principles', dismissing the gods as a product of human thought and convention. While we should not put her in that camp, the emphasis on this theme in the play (see 1080) and its embodiment in the dramatic plan would not have been lost on the Greek audience. If Oedipus had no regard for the gods, he would never have gone to Delphi and would not still fear its oracle (992).

1012 Here, as regularly, the Greek avoids explicit reference to *incest*, saying rather 'pollution from your parents'.

1022 Not the least 'chance' in the play derives from the fact that this messenger was once a shepherd who saved the infant Oedipus and delivered him to the house of Polybus.

1036 With *this* understand 'chance'; his *name* means Swellfoot.

1052 By *peasant* the choral leader refers to the slave who accompanied Laius, witnessed his murder, and requested that he be sent to the country.

1056 Some readers have felt that Jocasta has realized the secret of Oedipus' identity much earlier. Clearly, she now does.

1063 As ever, Oedipus too quickly jumps to a conclusion, this time misunderstanding Jocasta's fear.

1076 The *silence* is unexplained. If they actually hear nothing, that can only be attributed to her speech being an aside, addressed to the audience rather than to either the chorus or Oedipus.

1077 Caught up in the latest news, Oedipus for the moment forgets the murder of Laius.

1080 *Fortune*: see 262, 777 ('chance'), and 977. Of course, the wheel of fortune comes round, and Oedipus is too ready to see only luck, whereas the careful Greek sees both good and bad luck under the same sign.

1087–1117 Oedipus remains on stage while the chorus sings hopefully of the possibilities of divine birth for their king.

1091 *Sky* translates Olympus.

1094 Since Mount Cithaeron is in part Theban, if Oedipus was born there, he will be a *native* son.

1098 Possible fathers are listed: *Pan* is the rustic goat god, seldom a father of heroes; *Loxias* is Apollo; *Cyllene's king* is Hermes; the *Bacchants' God* is Dionysus. *Helicon* is another mountain of Boeotia, famed for its association with the Muses.

1153–4 *Pain* and *hurt* point to the use of torture, which Athenian law not only permitted but required of slaves giving evidence in court (it was supposed they would be more truthful under torture).

1167 The Greek for *children of Laius* may mean 'children of the house of Laius'.

1186–1223 In the fourth stasimon the chorus laments the fall of Oedipus, who is taken as an heroic paradigm of the human lot. Many of the motifs here are as old as Homer and Hesiod, but the figure of their ruined king is ever before them.

1186–96 The Greek does not equate man's life to the dead but sees life as a nothingness or as coming to nothing. *Turning away* =

'declining'. The Greek translated *pattern* gives us 'paradigm'. *Fate* is *daimôn* (see on 816 and cf. 1301). *Happiness* (1191 and 1199) play on this (*eudaimôn*).

1201 The *maid* is the Sphinx.

1205 *Fate* might also be translated 'ruin'.

1214 The Greek is more euphemistic than *accursed* may sound; though the deeds are unspeakable, the chorus is sympathetic.

1222–3 For *lull my mouth to sleep* read 'close my eyes in sleep'.

1224 This *Messenger* is a household slave, which explains how he is able to speak as a witness of what has happened within.

1227 The *Phasis* river flows into the eastern part of the Black Sea. The *Ister* is the Danube.

1245 After *hands* the translation has omitted a line: 'when she entered, she slammed the doors shut'. Without this line the text is relieved of a contradiction, but there is no other reason to suspect it. Here and below the translator has turned the servant's indirect report to direct speech.

1264 The epic translation (*Odyssey* ll. 277–8) made her a suicide from *hanging*.

1270 Our first evidence for his self-blinding is found in Aeschylus' *Seven against Thebes*.

1298–1366 Most of this passage is in lyric meters.

1301 *Evil spirit* (*daimôn*) is the same as 'some god' (1259) and 'Spirit' (1311). Early Greek psychology and Attic tragedy looked for an external cause for madness and aberrant behavior. Double causation is not uncommon, as at 1329–35.

1382 Although the play began as a *criminal* investigation, the language here and elsewhere tends to emphasize the cursed, unholy (*impure*) nature of his acts. So, too, 'guilt' (1384) is better 'taint' (as it was rendered at 833); incest and parricide have made him a pollution on the land (1427).

1439 In these extraordinary circumstances Creon intends to consult Delphi once more (see 1515 ff.).

1458 It is hard to know, specifically, what Oedipus has in mind by *strange evil fate*.

1461 His *sons* are Eteocles and Polyneices (see the *Antigone*). His daughters Antigone and Ismene are surely not expected by the audience, any more than Creon's postponement of a final decision on Oedipus' future is.

1520–21 The meaning of these lines is muddled, and it is not clear what happens. Taplin (pp. 45–6) thinks Oedipus goes into the palace; many critics write as if he goes off into exile – but why should Creon's decision be annulled so suddenly?

1524–30 Some editors condemn these lines, which are not altogether coherent. The chorus usually but not always has the final word, and these commonplaces are not atypical. Lines 1524–5 are virtually the same as those at *Phoenician Women* 1757–8.

OEDIPUS AT COLONUS

1 *Oedipus the King* begins with 'children'; the first word here is *child*.

9 *High breeding* will be 'nobility' in later passages; cf. 86, 648, 1195, and 1857. The theme will be elaborated more in ethical than in political terms.

40–44 The first dramatic complication derives from this accidental resting in a sacred precinct.

46 The place belongs to the *Eumenides* (the 'Kindly Ones' at 543); they are addressed in prayer at 95–122. In their malevolent aspect they are known as Erinyes (=Furies, as at 1639; see on 1488). These spirits of vengeance, often associated with a curse, are known to Hesiod and Homer and compose the chorus in Aeschylus' *Eumenides*. See *Antigone* 1146.

51–2 Apollo's oracle spoke not of Colonus but of the Furies (see 99–103). This is one of several suppliant dramas among the surviving tragedies. A victim and vulnerable, the suppliant puts himself under the power of the god, either at an altar or in a sanctuary, and thereby gains for himself the power of the god's protection. As the stranger sees it, Oedipus has violated the place, and the folk of Colonus will feel this all the more keenly when they know who he is; at the same time, however, he has put himself in the hands of these divinities, and it is their business to deal with him as they will.

55 *What I am doing* should be 'what you are doing'.

64–8 *Prometheus* stole fire from the gods and gave it to man. At Athens torch races were held in his honor. The *Bronze Road* was probably associated with an entrance to the underworld; see 1811–18. *Colonus* means 'hill'; the hero took his name from the place.

78 The popular hero *Theseus* also appears in Euripides' *Heracles* where he offers sanctuary to that hero.

82 This is the first allusion to the suppliant's usefulness; see 105, 301, 451–8, 503, and 513–14.

99 *Those horrors* are apparently the oracles of Apollo (*Phoebus*) pertaining to Laius and Jocasta. The earlier plays give us no reference for lines 100–108.

105–6 Like the Furies themselves, the dead, heroized Oedipus will be a power for good and harm. *Curse* (*atê*) is elsewhere ruin/ destruction (*Ant.* 666); at 207 it is perhaps too weak as 'mischief'.

112 The usual drink offering (libation) contains some wine, but the Eumenides/Furies receive an offering of milk, honey, and water (165–6). Oedipus' sobriety (*dry-mouthed*) is perhaps proleptic, to be attributed to participation in their rites.

128 Sophocles seems to have conceived Oedipus' character as a kind of oxymoron: the powerful victim, the truculent suppliant, the imperious beggar here calls for *caution*. The hiding has the dramatic virtue of offering, through the first strophe, a narrower focus on the character of the agitated chorus.

129 After the first strophe (129–43) the parodos takes the form of a lyric scene, with more dialogue, argument, and action than we normally find at this point. Antigone's role (she sings the final section) expands the scene and foreshadows a more significant role for her, and for Ismene.

161 As they think only of his blindness and do not yet know who he is, there is keen irony in *curse* (see on *OK* 246).

207 The exclamation seems a non sequitur. Perhaps the thought of his dependence prompts it, as if the gloomy ruin of his life cannot be gone.

228 The *Labdacids* are the family of Labdacus, grandfather of Oedipus.

248 Superstitiously, they cannot speak of his pollution but instead refer to the taint he carries as a *debt*. Parricide and incest attach such a stain that no house or place is safe from the pollution they carry.

263 This kind of retrospective religious moralizing is very common in Greek literature. See on *Antigone* 1349.

278–9 Antigone has already suggested that he acted in ignorance (252); twice later (584–6 and 1108–13) he will elaborate this argument; and self-defense was a legitimate argument in Athenian courts. But incest is another matter, so that *Even had I done what I did fully consciously* (283) can only apply to the death of

Laius. Lines 286–7 would seem to go so far as to blame his parents for failing to kill him when he was a baby.

Such passages pose a familiar kind of problem in Attic tragedy, which, with one exception in extant drama, takes its plots from traditional myths. Those myths carry religious and social values that were gradually qualified by later cultural institutions. By the fifth century poets had not only a number of versions for the same story but also multivalenced motifs and themes ready to combine in far greater variety than was available in our earliest tales. For example, in *Oedipus the King* neither Oedipus nor any other agent can imagine circumstances extenuating his actions, while in this play he invokes arguments, anachronistic in terms of the mythic time of the *OK*, which contemporary jurors might have found exculpating. This is not to say that in its values *Oedipus the King* is primitive (the legal process of that play is thoroughly modern), or that Greek myth and literature reveal some sort of simple 'progress' in religion and justice. In this regard we have only to note that our earliest evidence for this story reports that Oedipus stayed on as king after his crimes had been revealed (that is, for the poets of epic the pollution seems not to have been a compelling factor). For another conflict of this type see on 398–410.

289–90 *Beseech* renews the suppliant's plea; *took me* refers to the gesture of raising the suppliant and thereby accepting his plea.

300–301 *Benefit*: see on 82 and 657–8. It is not clear whether this claimed holiness derives from the (fulfilled) oracles of Apollo or from the protection offered him by the Eumenides.

306 *Haunted* interprets; it seems as likely that *thoughts* simply refers to his argument.

311 Theseus' *father* is Aegeus. From the following dialogue we would expect Theseus. Instead, Antigone descries Ismene (327), and the large role already given Antigone is enhanced by the second sister with news from Thebes.

330–35 *Etnean*: Sicilian, from Mount Etna on that island. *Thessalian* hats were broad-brimmed. Since the actors wore masks, descriptions like *her eyes are all aglow* are often found in introductory passages by way of suggesting the attitude of the speaker or, more commonly, the demeanor of the arriving character (see 826, 1435–6, and *OK* 80–84).

342 Ismene fulfills a messenger's functions (news of the brothers

[395 ff.], oracles [423 ff.] and Creon's advent [439]), but as a member of the family her dramatic value can be considerably extended.

345–58 Here the Greek offers seven lines divided between speakers. This technique (the technical term is *antilabe*) is often used in emotionally charged passages.

365 The example of *Egypt* may be taken from Herodotus (2.35). Oedipus' alienation from his sons Eteocles and Polyneices is already present in Aeschylus' *Seven against Thebes*. In that play, as here, the boys have failed to care for their father properly (the specific offense is not clear), for which Oedipus has cursed them, as he will curse them here (see 1564–76). Under Athenian law, mistreatment or neglect of parents was actionable; cf. his 'dishonored' at 477, in a passage implicating his sons in his suffering. Here the expanded role for the daughters provides a dramatic counterpoise to the failures of the sons. *Nature* (cf. 217 and 281) and *how they live* (= *means to live*, 382) are marked thematic terms in this play. Ismene picks up the latter idea at 393 (where *and how you were living*).

397 Ismene calls her brothers *unhappy*, a stock word rendered 'doomed' at 235 but still indicating more sympathy than Oedipus has to offer.

398–408 At first the boys, as sons of an incestuous union (*pollute*), refused succession. Then a rivalry for power developed, natural enough for boys sometimes represented as twins, and in all versions represented as bitter rivals. Considered in a religious and social light, the curse and pollution should have acted as an absolute interdiction. The double motivation (*god and sinfulness*) is typical of the religious and psychological perspective of tragedy (see 1490 ff.). The *younger* is Eteocles.

414 Polyneices' rally gathered the 'Seven against Thebes'.

419–20 Ismene's last sentence seems to assume her father will be troubled by the quarrels of his sons, but he ignores the substance of her report to ask after his own lot, which leads to the oracles.

429–30 Oedipus' skepticism here (cf. 433–4) contradicts his confidence at 300–301. Cf. 456.

432 *Victory* translates a stem very nearly overworked in these pages: it occurs at 407 (of political power; cf. 500), 445 ('to own you' = 'to control you'; again at 456), and 452 (in 'not as your own master'). The theme is power and control, and it is

prominent throughout the play (e.g., 738: 'I will conquer';
cf. 1576 and 1583).

435–6 *Exalt* = 'set you up', a metaphor from walking and travel that
Oedipus answers with 'they set right a poor old man who fell
when he was young' (437–8).

439 This line and 508 read like announcements of the imminent
arrival of Creon; Theseus will come and go first.

448–9 Another version: 'If your tomb chances to be unlucky (unluck-
ily situated) for them, it will be a heavy burden for them.'

450–51 As we shall see at the end of the play, the heroized dead are
thought to exert powerful influence from the grave (cf. 460).
Ritual tendance, however, was required if this power was to
remain effective. The Thebans wish to control the site of his
burial without risking pollution (454) arising from his presence
in their territory.

470 *Quarrel* = 'spirit of competition' (405).

481–94 This passage reads like a revision of the end of *Oedipus the King*,
where Oedipus vehemently desires exile but is held in Thebes
while Creon consults Delphi once again.

514 *Service* is repeated in 'savior' (517), another frequent thematic
word ('saving' at 544, 'safety' at 821 and 902; cf. 1281, 1289 and
1537). The theme's dramatic permutations virtually account for
the action.

521 One dramatic point of this *atonement* (purification) will be to take
Ismene off to make the sacrifice. Generally, the Greek stage
limited participation to three actors in any one scene; now
someone must leave to take the part of Theseus, and later of
Creon.

568–625 This section in the Greek is sung, more likely by Oedipus and
the *coryphaeus* (leader of the chorus) than by the full chorus.

588–90 Oedipus saved Thebes from the Sphinx, for which he was
given (610) the hand of the widowed queen. The metaphor in
bound goes back to Homer.

598 *Two curses* (*atê* in the plural): cf. *Ant.* 586, where Creon uses the
same phrase. The girls embody the ruining delusion he has
experienced. *Curse*, then, is not here literal, as, e.g., at 1569, but a
metonymic figure for them as the product of his fall.

602 Grene's interpretation implies that the playwright has introduced, if only latently, competing versions of the same myth.
While Athenian audiences will regularly have known variants,

often significant variants, to have introduced mutually exclusive facts in the manner he suggests produces a metatheater foreign to fifth-century convention. On the other hand, to exhibit a chorus seeking firsthand knowledge from an agent is familiar enough. They know by report, he can tell them the personal truth.

623–4 The text of 623 is uncertain. *Innocent* means 'pure', a personal and revisionist view (cf. 1299–1306).

628 Theseus comes well disposed (635 marks his recognition of Oedipus' suppliant status), ready to learn what he may do for Oedipus.

640 Theseus was born in *exile* at Troizen and as a young man came to Athens looking for his father; along the way he disposed of several local monsters.

645 For the motif only *a man* see *Ajax* 124–6 and Euripides, *Heracles* 1311–21 (Theseus speaks to Heracles).

657 For the thematic *gains* see on 82. Oedipus promises a real advantage in the future (738); salvation for him brings salvation for the city (690 and 719).

678 Here and at 654 Theseus' language suggests 'instruct me'.

691 Given the prolonged Peloponnesian War and the intensity of Theban animosity toward Athens, this must be one of the most naive questions in Greek tragedy.

693–710 Discourse on *time* and mutability is frequent in tragedy and lyric poetry. See 8, 659 and 1668; cf. *OK* 1077–86 and 1213.

721–8 Far from being an ally, Oedipus does not seem, at 74–7, to know anything of the city. Nor does there appear to be anything in earlier stories that would connect Theseus and Oedipus by ties of *guest-friendship*. In positing this relationship Theseus lays ground ready for making Oedipus a *citizen*, which responds to the request of 713–15.

738–9 *Conquer* recalls the theme of power (see on 432) while *gift* rings a change on the bitter gift of Jocasta (610), 'favor' (666), 'worth-less' (716), and 'recompense' (725).

740–52 Having received all he wanted, Oedipus lapses into anxiety. Theseus' departure and the arrival of Creon will, to some extent, justify his fears.

753 Theseus does not explain why he is leaving, and he does not return to Athens. With Antigone still on stage, he (i.e., the actor) must depart to take the role of Creon (see on 521).

765–813 Addressed to Oedipus, the first stasimon is devoted to praise of Athens. For such lyric praise cf. *Medea* 824–45.

775 When *Dionysus* was saved from the womb of Semele, he was sown in the thigh of Zeus; later Zeus gave him to the nymphs of Mount Mysa (his *nurses*) to raise. For extensive praise of this god see *Ant.* 1193–1225.

779–82 The *Great Goddesses* are probably Demeter and Persephone. The *Cephisus* and the Ilissus are the two best-known rivers of Attica.

788 The ornamental *Golden Reins* probably looks to the chariot of Aphrodite; it is used of other divinities.

792 The *island of Pelops* is the Peloponnesus.

796–801 The *olive* was Athena's gift to Athens when she and Poseidon contended for patronage of the city. Here it is the symbol of strength, independence, and fecundity. *Morian* regards Zeus as the god who watches over the sacred trees (olives dedicated to the god).

813 The *Nereids* ('daughters of Nereus') are sea nymphs, fifty in number, not grotesque multipeds.

825 Creon wants to persuade Oedipus to return to Thebes, but Ismene has been brought on previously, so that the audience and Oedipus know he lies. While Ismene's revelations may somewhat undercut one kind of tension (had Oedipus been deceived, how would he have been undeceived?), the show of force promises another (Theseus is away; will he return in time?).

835–6 What exactly is the status of Creon? It would seem from 398–410 that Eteocles has assumed power, while at 977 Creon describes himself as *turannos* ('sovereign lord'). Here he may, to ingratiate, suggest a more democratic mission than is the case. Yet what of Eteocles? On some of the issues involved see (carefully) Vidal-Naquet, 'Oedipus Between Two Cities'.

863 Oedipus knows from Ismene's report (444–9) that Creon has no intention of taking him back to Thebes (889–91). As if that were not enough to incite the exile, Creon concludes with *bred*, a word whose stem reminds Oedipus of the failure of his sons to care for their father (see on 365 and 'means to live').

884 *Grace* often involves a favor (666) done in return for something. Thematically, it is a matter of timely reciprocity.

893 A curse = 'spirit of revenge', an idea more common in Aeschylus than Sophocles. Oedipus has intuitions that after his death his spirit will prove a powerful daimonic presence; it is to this he refers.

913–14 The translation omits a taunt: 'you nurture the stain (that is your reproach)'. There seems to be a similar insult at 982. It is some measure of Oedipus' security that this aspersion on his polluted status evokes no more than an acid comment on Creon's sophistic skill.

923 The call for witnesses (cf. 1001) implies some legal standing for his claim. Yet he is a foreigner (see 1063–70). Antigone also appeals for witnesses (967).

928–30 Creon pretends to seize his own (the girls belong to his family and are Theban citizens; cf. 944, 949, and 1085), though his real motive is to secure hostages. It is not clear whether Ismene has already been taken or whether he now directs a guard to go for her.

943 Normally the actors are on a slightly elevated stage, the chorus below them in the orchestra. This rare (for Attic drama) physical violence requires a meeting of the antagonists, perhaps immediately in front of the stage.

977 If Creon is *turannos* (*sovereign lord*), and that means that he exercises political tyranny, then his earlier claims to represent the city are a bit fraudulent. Cf. Theseus' view of Thebes (1058–70).

1005 Creon has sent his guards off with the girls, a necessary step for the reappearance of Theseus, and also necessary to avoid armed violence, which we never find in the surviving plays.

1017 *Insolence* translates *hybris*, for which one could be brought to trial in Athens. Insult (as at 1104) as well as violence occasions charges of *hybris*, and aggrieved parties see themselves as mocked (cf. Theseus' indignation at 1040 and 1183, and Creon's at *Ant.* 524–7).

1053–5 At 75 we are told Athens is ruled by a king, while the description here is very much of fifth-century Athens.

1058 The following exculpation of *Thebes* has sponsored some subtle explanations (see Vidal-Naquet pp. 337–8). Note the choral approval (1078–80).

1090 The ancient Athenian court known as the *Areopagus* had as its chief province trials for homicide. In Aeschylus' *Eumenides* Orestes, who has killed his mother, is tried before its founding session. One great difference between Orestes and Oedipus is that the former has been purified at Delphi before coming to Athens. If Oedipus had ever received ritual purification, he would surely bring it up in response to Creon's present condemnation.

1104 Encore the arguments of 276–88 and 584–625, with nothing essential added, with more heat, and an immediate target for his invective. It is worth noting that Sophocles refuses to give Oedipus the kind of rationalizing, and humanizing, arguments found in Euripides' *Heracles* (see 1231–5) and *Orestes* (e.g., 395–400). His defense remains essentially legalistic (he did not intend to do what he did) and vaguely theological (1108–9 and 1147–8).

1109–12 *Angry against my people of old* may allude to Laius' rape of Chrysippus, which would have been the ground for sexual interdictions in earlier versions of the story, though not in *Oedipus the King*. *Sins* is 'mistake/fault', as if to say, there is in me no fault for reproach so great as to explain the errors I have committed against myself. See on *Ant*. 972. Judging from its appearance five times in this speech, the idea of 'blame/reproach' dominates Oedipus' feeling.

1197 While Theseus secures the return of the girls, the chorus sings the second stasimon, which is largely devoted to imagining the fight and to praying for victory.

1200–1204 They think of two possible sites for the engagement, one near a temple of Apollo (*on Pythian shores*), the other at the sanctuary of Eleusis, where *torch-lighted* ceremonies were held to honor Demeter and Persephone (the *Sacred Ones*). *Golden key* refers metaphorically to the vow of silence imposed on initiates to their mysteries. The *Eumolpidae* clan provided priests for Eleusis.

1212 A third site, Mount *Oea*, is considered.

1225 Poseidon, brother of Zeus, is god of the sea and of horses, and the *son of Rhea* and Cronus. His praise at 803–13.

1248 Apollo's *sister* is Artemis, goddess of the hunt.

1256 The three speaking parts in this scene belong to Oedipus, Theseus, and Antigone. In another play we might expect a messenger to describe the victory, and Theseus could do that here but passes on because of the arrival of yet another player (1319–24).

1299–1306 Unexpectedly, these lines jerk us back to the issue of the polluted suppliant and exile. *Stain of evil* (as at *OK* 833 and 1384) recalls the old miasma, which Oedipus clearly fears is still potent, and which of course the men of Colonus rejected with fear and hostility when they first identified Oedipus. Modern efforts to make his reaction one of moral and psychological guilt hardly square with *touch* and its context here. Other interpreters seem to agree with Segal: 'Oedipus performs the lustral rites which purify the holy grove of his intrusion. Simultaneously he purifies himself of his pollution, both in words and in ritual deeds' (*Tragedy and Civilization* p. 385). Yet at this point only one ritual remains (1819–25), and that is a sacrifice to the dead; for Oedipus the earlier expiation does not, at this point, seem to have affected his pollution. Whatever the answer to this problem, it is worth noting that Theseus does not comment on it one way or the other.

1329 Polyneices has been cautious, taking the attitude of a suppliant and one requesting safe conduct (1340).

1342 *Argos*: see 412.

1358–60 Just as Oedipus' reception depended on pious regard for the suppliant, so now he must consider whether he too is not bound by the same sacral rules.

1361 Once again we see the larger role designed for Antigone, whose appeal strongly resonates with notions of duty and reciprocity pervasive in the play.

1394 Theseus departs; the actor taking his role will return as Polyneices.

1394–1434 The miseries of old age, a commonplace in Greek poetry, here inspired by Oedipus' alienation from his sons.

1403 *Into that region ... term* = 'beyond a due length of life'. In the Greek the *Helper* is immediately clarified by 'the lot/fate of life', i.e., the lot owed Hades.

1451–5 Both *food* and *supporting him* remind the auditor, and Oedipus, of a theme enunciated vehemently at 365–91. In what follows Oedipus may seem to the modern reader brutally harsh; it cannot be stressed too much that, for the Greeks, Eteocles and Polyneices have committed a cardinal sin in their failure to care for their father.

1457 *Mercy (aidôs)* is usually rendered Shame (cf. 577, 993), an inhibitory compunction that might, he hopes, keep his father from treating him as he deserves.

1459 *Why are you silent?* is a part-line in the Greek, no doubt with a strong pause to mark Oedipus' obduracy.

1486–9 *The city which he persuaded* is another phrase throwing some uncertainty over the governance of Thebes. *Curse* = Erinys (Fury), the spirit invoked by his father's vengeful curses. Polyneices, of course, cannot know of his father's recent curse (470–76).

1494 *Apian land* from the legendary founder Apius.

1503–13 This list of captains is the same found in Aeschylus, *Seven against Thebes* (376–626, in which each is described and an opponent is nominated by Eteocles). *Amphiareus* is a famous seer. *Atalanta* is best known for taking part in the Calydonian boar hunt. Her son's name (*Parthenopaeus*) means 'son of a maiden'. This expedition came to a bad end, and its failure is the background for the *Antigone*.

1521 These *oracles* may be his own (1489) or those that Ismene reported. On yielding (1525) see *Ant.* 1168 and 1177.

1533–4 While much in this speech must be sincere, however self-serving, one wonders if he can bring Oedipus home, if he really means to. That was not Creon's commission.

1537 Or: 'I have no strength to be saved.' Now that Oedipus has sanctuary and has been saved from Creon, it his turn to save or deny. Recent thematic words at 1281 and 1289.

1548–50 The sequence of events leading to Colonus and the roles played by Creon, the brothers, and the city are not clear, perhaps because everyone, especially Oedipus, has a passionate interest in a different truth. For example, compare his account at 476–80, where he talks as if the brothers simply stood by while the city drove him out (490–92). Other passages related to these antecedents will be found at 398–410, 683–5, and 1480–89.

1555–6 *Remembering* you as *my murderer*. The 'you' is explicit. *Rearing* and *nurses* (1559 and 1561) are emphatically placed reminders of the theme elaborated at 365–91.

1564 *The Evil Spirit has eyes* = 'the daimon watches'. As we approach the heroization of Oedipus himself, the supernatural has a larger place in the language (daimon is 'lot' at 1528; 'spirits' at 1590; 'Fortune' at 1658; 'God' at 1693).

1568–9 *Polluted*: cf. *Ant.* 190. The *curses* he now formally pronounces were before this given at 470–76. *Days gone by* freely renders what might be 'previously'. The audience knows the legend in which the brothers kill one another before the gates of Thebes. Cf. 1585.

1578 This personification responds to that at 1457. Cf. *Ant.* 495.

1606–12 The passage refers, rather heavily perhaps, to the action of the *Antigone*, written over thirty-five years earlier.

1662 Each strophe and antistrophe is followed by five lines of iambic dialogue, until the arrival of Theseus interrupts before the last set of five. The first strophe seems to allude to Oedipus' curses, and then to wonder if some earlier *Fate* (I would not personify)

has surfaced. In his first speech *Time* was grouped with suffering
and nobility as his teachers (7–9).

1671 A tympany may have been used for the *thunder* but it is hard to
imagine realistic lightning (1681) in the Greek theater. These
signs are traditionally associated with Zeus, whose weapons in
battle are lightning bolts.

1691 Fearing for itself and thinking Oedipus the cause of this terror,
the chorus prays to the daimon (*God*) that it may not be
implicated in his fate. Then, at 1703–4, reminded by Oedipus of
the favor he has promised, it returns to the favor (1709–11) and
joins in a prayer for Theseus' prompt appearance, which is
answered. *Now is duly paid* (1704) is clearer as 'now duly to pay'.

1745–8 The actual place of burial will remain a secret, closely guarded
by an hereditary priesthood. While there is no pre-Sophoclean
evidence for a cult of Oedipus at Colonus, this final scene
suggests that Sophocles has invested some actual rite with the
aetiological value of a founder's myth.

1750 *The Sown Men* are the Spartoi who descended from the teeth of
the dragon sown by Cadmus. The next sentence seems to pose
Theban aggression as a remote possibility.

1765 *Hermes* conducts the souls of the dead to Hades. The *goddess of the
dead* is *Persephone*, queen of the underworld, consort of Hades; she
is the *Goddess Unseen* of 1775.

1774–85 This prayer is addressed to Persephone and the *Aidoneus*,
another name for Hades. For the Greeks the underworld is the
destiny of all the dead, not a place of punishment, save for a few
legendary misfits. The Styx (*Stygian*) is a river of the underworld,
famous because the gods take their oath by it.

1786–91 The *goddesses* are the Furies. The *Hound* is Cerberus, the three-
headed dog who guards the gates of the underworld.

1792 The *son of Earth and Tartarus* is probably Death, brother of *Sleep*
in Greek myth.

1811–18 See on 64–8. The manner of this description implies these
were familiar landmarks to Sophocles' audience. The context as
well as the reference to *Peirithous* marks this place as an entrance
to the underworld. Theseus and Peirithous made a pact to have
daughters of Zeus for brides. When Peirithous chose Persephone, the two heroes went down to Hades to carry her off.

1822 For *Demeter* see on 1201–4. She is connected with agriculture, the
dead (through Persephone), and the mysteries of Eleusis.

1852–7 *Oedipus the King* concludes with the king committing his daughters to the care of Creon (1504–10). *Noble*: see on 9 and cf. 1862.

1893   The messenger departs. A lament in lyric meters follows. What has seemed to many modern readers mysteriously inspiring is for the girls an occasion for mourning.

1897   *Curse*: as at 1697 and 606, where 'What I can never forget' is true to the etymology; it seems that the unlucky family, rather than murder and incest, defines the referent.

1917   *Living* returns a lively theme (notes at 365, 863, 1451).

1920   *Murdering Hades* is rather strong for 'bloody/deadly'.

1961–2   Perhaps Ismene's seemingly obtuse question is sponsored by the allusiveness of 'to see the hearth of earth' (=*where he lies in earth*). Hearth suggests both home and altar (place of sacrifice).

1992   *The Underworld Gods*='the night of the world below'. *Grace* (favor/requital/benefit) has appeared frequently: 666, 884, 1698, 1703, 1711, and finally in 2017.

2009–10   *The God*=a daimon (Fate at 1991). *Zeus* holds those who take oaths to their word, or is supposed to.

2013   A final allusion to their presence in Thebes during and after the seige of Polyneices' army.

ANTIGONE

1   Her speech strongly emphasizes shared ties of family and interest. The most ancient traditions of Greek poetry attribute both *evils* and prosperity to the gods, even when there is no directly personal interest of the deity (*Zeus*).

9   The *commander* is Creon, her uncle and the new regent. He will expound the *proclamation* in his first speech.

11–12   Goldhill's reading of the play (pp. 88–106) focuses on language and action pertaining to friends and foes. Her brother Polyneices has led an army against his brother Eteocles and his native Thebes. For this Polyneices has been condemned as a traitor and treated as a common enemy (211–15).

17   Polyneices had raised an army in Argos. See Aeschylus' *Seven against Thebes* for the posting of the two brothers to the same gate where they died in hand-to-hand combat. See *OC* 1490 ff., and 156–62 below. *In this past night* may also mean 'in the present night', and the predawn darkness explains the ease with which Antigone accomplishes the first burial. Cf. 118–21 and 253.

28 *Lawful rites* points to the customs and conventions of burial, not to written law. Denial of burial was invoked only against the worst crimes; Creon thinks of Polyneices as guilty of treason and intending tyranny (221). For a brief historical perspective see W. K. Lacey, *The Family in Classical Greece*, Cornell University Press, 1968, p. 80.

35 Leaving a foe for dogs and *birds* is a motif as old as the *Iliad*. See 225 and Sophocles' *Electra* 1487–8 and *Ajax* 830. Ritual burial gives the dead spirit leave to pass on to the underworld; burial in the bowels of birds and dogs shames the dead and dishonors the family.

47 Antigone has already resolved to bury her brother.

55–62 Of the three Theban plays, *Antigone* was the first produced; hence we cannot look to the *Oedipus the King* for background. In this play there is no indication that Oedipus ever left home. His wife and mother Jocasta hanged herself.

66–78 The prologue repays comparison with *Electra* 938–1057, where Electra attempts to persuade her sister Chrysothemis to join her in avenging their father. For the argument that a woman cannot *fight against men* see *Electra* 996–7. Ismene never denies that religious and moral right is with Antigone.

81–3 *Be as you choose to be* may also mean 'think what you like'. *Good* suggests 'noble/fair', i.e., what brings a good name. Cf. 114 where the same stem is negated in 'ignobly'. This line of argument perhaps seemed less morbid to the Greeks: the family had primary responsibility, better obligation, for burial, for tendance of the grave, and for preservation of cult and worship at the grave. Ismene turns her back on the most profound of duties, while Antigone's determination to *please* the *dead* (86) marks her as one fulfilling the family's natural and honorable claims on any survivor. On Athenian sentiment about burial and family cult see Lacey pp. 147–9.

96 *Make straight your own path to destiny* suggests something like our 'set your own house in order'.

109–10 *Loathe* and *enemy* are from the same stem as 'enemies' in line 11.

116–17 *Friends* and *love* are the same word in different grammatical forms, and 'love' may sometimes suggest sentimental and romantic notions foreign to the Greek, which includes a large enough field for the sentry (a household slave) to use it of Antigone (482). 'Dear to your friends' is the meaning.

118–78 In this translation choral passages are not always paragraphed according to the Greek antiphonal parts (strophe and anti-strophe). The chorus (Theban elders summoned by Creon) celebrates the previous day's victory over the Argive army.

122–4 *Dirce* is a well-known river near Thebes. The shields of the Argives were plain.

142 The Theban aristocracy traced its origins to the men (Spartoi) who sprang from the teeth of the *dragon* killed by the founder Cadmus.

143–9 The insolent boaster is Capaneus, who swore that not even Zeus would keep him from sacking the city; for which Zeus struck him with lightning.

155 *Wheel horse* likens Ares (the god of war) to the hard-working, righthand horse in the team of four.

158–9 *Their brazen suits of armor*: they dedicate their victorious arms to Zeus who gave them victory.

169 *Bacchus*: for a hymn to this god see 1193 ff.

172 *Creon* is the brother of Jocasta, wife of Oedipus; in some versions he was regent during the minority of the brothers.

179 Just as Antigone's decision is rooted in Greek values of family and religion, and should not be read as purely personal and idiosyncratic, so Creon may also be seen as more than a melodramatic tyrant. Kells ('Problems of Interpretation in the *Antigone*, Bulletin of the Institute of Classical Studies, University of London 10 (1963),' p. 60) is closer to the mark: 'he is filled with the commonplace ideas of his day – that the state is above everything, that military virtue is the supreme virtue, that women are inferiors, that sons owe unquestioning obedience to their fathers; above all, that a man – a gentleman – should see friends and enemies everywhere, and devote a considerable portion of his energy to the discomfiture of the latter'. Creon has as good a case against Polyneices as the Athenians had against Themistocles, of whom Thucydides reports: 'It is said that his bones were, at his desire, brought home by his relations and buried secretly in Attica. The secrecy was necessary since it is against the law to bury in Attica the bones of one who has been exiled for treason' (l. 138). From Homer on the poetic tradition makes the right to burial a lively topic; for an example, see Sophocles' *Ajax* 1049 ff. Creon's measures and manner are extreme (see 1152–6), and the play condemns him, but it will be some time before the Theban elders offer a decisive judgment.

185 *Laius* is the father of Oedipus.

190 They are *defiled* because they have shed kindred blood.

204 Zeus (*God*) is invoked as the god of oaths (see 335–6).

217–21 He stresses that this attack threatened their homes and the temples and images of the gods; cf. 312–20.

225 *Violated* suggests shameful mutilation.

230–33 In matters of friendship and morality Sophoclean choruses are usually found on one side or the other. For a good part of the play this chorus is cautious, pragmatic, and noncommittal.

244 *Lay-by in my thinking* is one of several turns that mark the guard as a self-conscious caricature of the tragical-historical style. At first Creon humors him (259 and 263–4).

270 In the view of this witness the necessary *ritual*, symbolic rites that would placate the dead, is completed. See 282–3.

282 In the Greek the guard's *avoiding the curse* may suggest that someone, inspired by fear of the unconsecrated dead, has scattered dust to avoid pollution. See Robert Parker, *Miasma* Clarendon Press, 1983, p. 8.

286 The *bad words* are 'abuse', and not a piece in his tragical posturing.

308–9 Some modern readers have taken this and other bits of evidence (e.g., 273–7 and 458–64) as signs that the gods really did attend to the burial, which would explain Antigone's second trip to the site. But it would be curious if some divine agency had troubled to perform the ritual and had not truly protected the body (see 453, 1072–4, and 1279).

310 The exasperated Creon assumes a conspiracy for personal gain, as does Oedipus when Teiresias is not forthcoming (*OK* 380 ff.).

362–7 Either the guard's final comment is an aside, or Creon exits at the end of his speech (361), and the guard's parting shot is unheard by the king.

368–411 In this first stasimon the chorus ponders the strange thing called man, his triumphs and his limits. While much in its imagery and metaphor is knotted into the play (see Segal, chapter 6), it lacks immediate and direct dramatic import, but then the chorus does not yet know that it is Creon's own niece who has asserted her justice and law opposed to his. The first strophe treats man's triumph over the physical world; the first antistrophe describes his conquest of animals; the second strophe (387–99) turns to intellectual, political, and medical achievement; and the second antistrophe balances praise for human craft with a warning that political prosperity requires regard for divine and human law.

387 The *wind* may suggest what is quick, lofty, changeable, unstable. *Tempers that go with city living*: Jebb translates 'such dispositions as regulate cities', but as in the previous figure an undertow implies passion/temper.

404 With *laws* the sentence seems to affirm Creon's position (195, 210, 232), but Antigone has also invoked law (28; cf. 494 ff.).

435 *Grace of burial* signifies tendance and cleaning of the corpse (cf. 472–5).

449 Sweeping away the dust cannot undo the ritual which they recognize has already taken place, so the point would seem to be an abuse of the corpse that, they hope, will offend its friends and bring them out of cover.

464 Phrases such as *sent by the gods* need not be taken literally, though some critics have done (see on 308–9).

470–71 *Stripped* might be the guard's word, but her *curse* on those *that had done that deed* is most naturally taken as denoting her reaction to their interference in her rites, which of course means that it was she who came in the predawn hours and scattered the dust. Why does she come here a second time? Perhaps for purely personal reasons, from a desire to mourn and to protect the exposed body. Perhaps Sophocles thought to telescope Athenian ritual, which required offerings to the dead on the third and ninth days after burial. Whatever the reason, no one in the play finds it remarkable.

494–5 Since Hesiod *Justice* has been a daughter of *Zeus*. She *lives with* (the gods) *below* because the rights of the dead are at issue. With Aristotle we would call the argument one from natural law, or from the conventions that bind and define cultural usage. It takes up the first half of her speech; at 504 she takes a more personal turn, fully defiant, and it is to the second half that the coryphaeus (515–17) and Creon respond.

499 *God's* should read gods'. Sometimes *theos* and its plural refer to specific divinities, as often not. Capitalization is often arbitrary, and there is a tendency to substitute singulars for plurals (e.g., in 807 and 978).

517 Refusal to *yield* is characteristic not only of Antigone but of most Sophoclean protagonists; cf. 774, 1169 and 1177, and see Knox, *Heroic Temper* pp. 15–17.

524–7 Charges of pride, *insolence* (hybris), and boasting are stock motifs in tragic polemic. Cf. Agamemnon's speech at *Ajax* 1224 ff. We probably don't learn much from this tirade about Antigone's actual manners.

547 *Glory* may seem a different tact from the piety of 494 ff., but she thinks of the reputation/good report derived from doing the right thing. See the choral praise at 878–84.

553–6 Since Greek choruses do defy tyrants, usurpers, and assassins – the last scene of the *Agamemnon* is a celebrated example – we should not suppose that dramatic convention rather than dramatic purpose keeps them silent now. Haemon will make similar suggestions about popular feeling (744–9), and the chorus itself will finally admonish Creon (1175).

562–9 Nothing in the stories or dramatic representations of the brothers implies anything other than radical, personal hatred, which, however, only shows that Antigone is not viewing the situation from the perspective of tradition. For a similar hypothetical argument see *OC* 1148–9.

575–6 Creon's view is traditional; cf. *OC* 190–92 and *Electra* 1487–90. In Antigone's *love* is found the stem that has been 'friend' throughout the play (see on 116–17). It appears in 603, where the meaning 'what is dear' permits us to translate 'How can life be worthwhile without you?' In popular morality, helping friends was as much the rule as hurting enemies.

586 By a common metonymy the girls are identified with the effect they cause (*destruction*).

592–602 In rejecting Ismene's late support Antigone shows a harsher side than some readers like; hence one line of interpretation argues she is trying to save her sister.

606 A controversial line: if Antigone means that she regrets her sarcasm, then it is virtually the only line in the play in which Antigone extends such sympathetic understanding to another. Kells argues that Antigone suffers because she realizes her taunt (604) is, practically speaking, a dismissal of Ismene from her house. On this view Ismene has lost her place in the family because she has refused to support it; in so doing she has made herself one to be mocked, an enemy, not a friend.

626–7 *Your son's* refers to Haemon and foreshadows his apperance in the next scene (686). *Fields for him to plough*: similar language appears in legal contracts for marriage and in a variety of poetic contexts.

630–34 The manuscripts attribute 630 to Ismene, the majority of modern editors assign it to Antigone. The issue is interpretative rather than textual: Ismene has introduced the topic of their marriage and may be expected to follow her own argument; on the other hand, Antigone is engaged to Haemon, whose love for her will motivate his subsequent actions. If she loves him, this is the only line that expresses that love. While there is more pathos in assigning the line to Antigone, her tone in this scene hardly seems shaped for romantic effusion.

635 *Both you and I have decided it* = 'It is determined, for both of us.' That is, there will be no arguing the decision.

640–78 The second stasimon meditates on the miseries of the family. Apart from the reference to Labdacus and Oedipus, there is little here specific to this house, much that is commonplace in its morality and theology, and nothing that offers a peculiar view of recent events.

648 *Labdacus* is the grandfather of Oedipus. For the sentiment compare

> Old is the tale of sin I tell
> but swift in retribution
> to the third generation.
>
> (*Seven against Thebes* 742–4)

While we may tend to see the play as a confrontation between two strong personalities, the Greek audience may have felt that passages like 515–17 and 911–21 and the implication of Haemon, Eurydice and even Megareus (1379) in Creon's catastrophe focus as much on the divided, cursed house as on its individuals.

655–6 'Dust cuts/harvests the root' (*mowed*) metaphorically refers to the burial. The personification of *folly* is common, and *ruin's enchantment* translates Erinys (Fury), a daimonic spirit of retribution well known since Homer. See 1146.

657 *Sin* = 'trespass', the 'over-stepping' we find at 498. *Sleep* is not usually thought of as weakening (*all-aging*), and the passage has been emended.

666 Strophe and antistrophe conclude with the same phrase (*without ruin* = *outside of calamity* [678]). For *atê* (ruin) see 586 ('destruction') and 1338.

667–78 *Hope* deludes and deceives because it leads men to ambition and risk beyond their powers; they forget that mutability is the first law of human affairs. Such a man confuses *good* and *evil*, and in the Greek view such a man's fall is yet another sign of the gods' power.

679 Haemon is Creon's youngest and last *son*. Though he comes to plead for Antigone's life, Sophocles gives him the second speech and the role of the wise counselor, until his father's obstinacy provokes him. The chorus wonders if he will play the romantic lover; their *cheated* (deceived) echoes 669 ('deceiver').

688–91 Natural ambiguities make *with your excellent judgment* also 'if your judgment is good' and *the goodness of your leadership* 'when/if your guidance is fair/noble'.

732–4 For Creon's views of women see 528, 578, 637, 808 and 820.

737 Haemon's tact makes him a dutiful son, a role calculated to persuade his father, and one which also minimizes the scope of romantic love in the play. The manner of his death brings different colors to light, but for now, knowing his father's temper, he takes a more politic line.

744–5 Cf. Antigone's opinion at 550–52.

764 *When opened up* is a metaphor from opening a letter or scroll.

809 *Yield to what is shameful* is not altogether clear. He would have acted shamefully if he refused to take up the burden of this argument. Perhaps he implies that his father has not kept so high a standard.

813–14 Creon takes *another* as a threat; Haemon grows more patient and may impetuously, and vaguely, refer to his own death.

825–7 What he suggests never actually happens on the Greek stage. The threat serves to motivate Haemon's immediate departure.

840–48 He modifies the original penalty of his edict (see 40–41). His reason for relenting just so much would seem based on the fear that killing someone in his own family might bring *pollution* (*miasma*) on himself and the city. See also 937–42. Giving her a bit to eat leaves her death to nature and Hades, who, he sardonically suggests, may answer her prayers.

849 After a pair of responsive stanzas (849–63) celebrating the power of love (in the Greek, *eros* is the first word, Aphrodite the last), Antigone enters to sing a lyric *kommos* (lament).

854 *Whose life is a day only* translates a single word, conventional for the brevity of human life; in English 'ephemeral'.

862–3 For the metaphor of fighting against Aphrodite see *Women of Trachis* 441–4, where other topics from the preceding lyric will also be found.

864 *Lawfulness* has just appeared in 861, where the translation, though free, seems fair. The Greek is commonly translated 'laws', with connotations of 'sacred/ancient'; while this is not the Greek word for law used earlier in our play (*nomos*), here, with the metaphor from racing, it may suggest that the sight of Antigone brings them to a more sympathetic appreciation of Haemon's reaction.

870 Several motifs in Antigone's lyrics belong to the vocabulary of popular as well as literary lament: *last road*, farewell to the *sun*, failure to marry, and bride of *Hades* (*Acheron* is one of the rivers of the underworld). Although she never mentions Haemon, in the dramatic context we must think of him; thus Sophocles maintains a kind of vague, teasing ambiguity in the matter of their mutual affection.

879 *Praise* reminds the audience of 'glory' (547) and 'glorious acts' (749). Cf. 894–6.

882 *It was your own choice* translates a single compound combining 'law' (*nomos*) and 'self' ('by a law you yourself have chosen'). Cf. 'self-willed' at 927.

885–91 The *daughter* is Niobe, who married Amphion, king of Thebes. For her boasting Apollo and Artemis killed her children, and she was transformed into a stone on Mount Sipylus in her native Phrygia. Antigone compares her own entombment to Niobe's, who still grieved and wept after she was turned to stone.

892 Tantalus (her father) was a son of Zeus, and Niobe shares that glory.

897 Why does she find mockery in their distinction? *Insult* is strong (from the *hybris* stem) and only be be found in 892–6 under extreme stress.

901 For *Dirce* see 122.

908–12 In this context *fell* seems to mean 'tripped over it in your *daring* enterprise', not a very consoling view. On the other hand, *requital for some ordeal of your father* asserts (the *perhaps* softens too much) that her death is an expiation of family sins, a familiar motif in myth and literature (see 642–56, *OC* 1109, and *Agamemnon* 1580–82); Antigone responds to this view, and the adjective 'cursed' (the *curse on me*, 921) assents to a fatalism which for us may sit uneasily with the assertion of personal responsibility (882 and 927). In Greek tragedy we commonly find double motivation, a kind of dual psychological model, in which both the

agents and the gods are held responsible. So, for example, at
1349 Creon says 'God has sprung on my head' when he and the
chorus have both just acknowledged his responsibility
(1339–41).

922 The *brother* is Polyneices, who married the daughter of Adrastus,
king of Argos, to secure an alliance and aid for his return to the
Theban throne.

939–42 For his thinking see on 840–48.

948 *Persephone* is queen of the underworld.

960–72 Because her argument/explanation seems to contradict prin-
ciple (particularly as stated at 494–503), these lines have been
condemned by some editors. From a religious perspective,
brother, *children* and *husband* are all one: burial of any member of
the family is imperative, and the possibility of replacing a child
or husband is immaterial. Various explanations have been
offered: in a typically Greek way she rationalizes feelings, i.e.,
attempts a practical reason for a personal attachment; or it is
argued that for a moment we witness the psychological stress of
imminent death breaking her will and defiance as she retreats to
lower ground. The chorus (987–8) emphasizes sameness rather
than any change in manner or substance.

972 *Criminal* is 'sin' at 983 and 'wrongdoer' at 984 (all are verbal
forms cognate with Aristotle's *hamartia*). Since this is not a
technical term for crime, and can be as innocuous as 'be
mistaken', she may be mocking Creon a bit. This is the vocabulary of 'mistake' at 1081 and 1340, and of 'false step' at 1330.

1002–41 In the fourth stasimon three stories of entombment or
imprisonment offer, allusively, parallels to Antigone's fate. The
connections seem more formal than telling. For a prudent survey
see Winnington-Ingram's examination (pp. 98–109).

1002 *Danaë* is the daughter of Acrisius, who, learning from an oracle
that his daughter's child would kill him, locked her up in
brassbound walls. Nonetheless, Zeus took the form of a *golden
shower* and got the child Perseus.

1012–21 The *son of Dryas* is Lycurgus, King of the Edonians, who
rashly rejected the worship of *Dionysus*. The *inspired women*,
elsewhere called Maenads and Bacchants, are the followers of the
god. *Drained away*: apparently of the gradual [dripping/trickling]
diminution of his madness, which Dionysus had caused. The
cultic cry (*euoi*) of the Bacchants is translated *fire*; cf. 1211.

1022–41 Cleopatra married *Phineus*, king of *Salmydessus* on the Black Sea. He put her away and married Idaea, who blinded the sons of Cleopatra. The savage god of these wild Thracians is Ares. *Looked vengefully* means their eyes cry out for vengeance. Cleopatra is the daughter of the god *Boreas* (the north wind) and Orithyia, princess of Athens (the *Erechteidae* are the descendants of Erechthus, a legendary king). That she was raised in a cave does not come to a close parallel with Antigone. Perhaps if we knew more of the two plays Sophocles composed about Phineus, the analogy would be more precise.

1042 For *Teiresias* see *OK* 300. There is no particular anticipation of his appearance, but his message bears out the views of Ismene and Haemon: Creon is in the wrong.

1056 Teiresias reads the will of the gods in the ways of birds. He also scans sacrificial offerings (1062–8). That the birds attack one another implies great disturbance in nature. The failure of the burnt offerings only corroborates the first evil auguries. The gods want no part of their sacrifice (1076–7), while the birds foul the altars with carrion from the battlefield.

1062 *Tasted* should be 'tested'.

1081–3 The point for Creon is that it is still possible to correct his mistake, as Teiresias' figure at 1050 already implies. *Accursed* is too strong for 'unfortunate'.

1094 He rebukes Teiresias for thinking that the king can be bought and sold; cf. 240–41, 1107 and 1118. Critics often blame Creon for blasphemy and irreligion. In this context, however, it is clearly his disbelief in Teiresias' auguries that prompts his vigor.

1104 We find the argument that no mortal can *pollute the gods* at Euripides' *Heracles* 1232. The theology is more recent than the mythic time of the play.

1115 *Sick*: for the metaphor cf. 792, 1072, and 1216.

1119 *Princes* classes Creon as a tyrant; *advantage* throws 'profit' (1107) back at him.

1123 For his help see 1379, where the reference to an older son of Creon probably alludes to a sacrifice meant to save the city. If Teiresias predicted, or called for, the sacrificial death of Creon's son, he is very bold to call that 'service' up now.

1145–6 The *Spirits of Death* probably defines *Furies*. Cf. 656 and *OC* 43–4.

1152–6 Only now is it revealed that Creon has denied burial to all the fallen dead. It was an Athenian boast that they had marched to Thebes and secured burial for the dead Argives (see Herodotus 9.27).

1168–71 *Curse (atê)* has been 'ruin' (666) and 'calamity' (678), which are better here. *To yield*: for the motif see on 517.

1178–9 Here too the idea is that Creon may yet avert disaster, which, practically, can only refer to some unstated consequence of Antigone's entombment.

1187–92 *Axes* (not mentioned later) are apparently needed for cutting wood for a funeral pyre. *The place you see, there* would be accompanied by a gesture, as if to a high plain where the body will be found. Line 1190 seems to mean his first thought is to free Antigone, but in fact he and his crew attend to the burial first. Perhaps the line only means 'What I've done I'll undo.' *The old accepted laws* refers to the conventions of religion and burial he has opposed.

1193–1225 The fifth stasimon optimistically celebrates Dionysus the healer. If disaster is avoided, as they hope, their native god will be responsible.

1193–1201 Dionysus (= *Bacchus*) is the son of Semele and Zeus. *Italy* has little to do with Dionysus; emendations have been offered. *Eleusis*, north of Athens, is the home of the mysteries presided over by Demeter (= *Deo*) and her daughter Persephone. For *dragon's teeth* see 142.

1202–14 The *twin peaks* rise above Delphi, below Mount Parnassus, with *Castalia* and the *Corycean* cave familiar landmarks at the oracle, where Dionysus shared honors with Apollo. Mount Nisaea is on Euboea (see on 1218). *Evoe* is the sound uttered by Bacchants as they summon their god. Semele (*mother*) was incinerated after she had persuaded Zeus to appear to her in all his glory (thunder and lightning, as it turned out).

1218 *Moaning strait* refers to the turbulent waters separating Euboea from the Boeotian coast.

1222–4 The *Thyiads* are, etymologically, the 'sacrificers', the women who attend to the rites of the god. *Iacchus* is both a shout invoking the god and a name for him.

1226 *Amphion*, husband of Niobe (886) and brother of Zethus, ruled Thebes during the minority and exile of Laius.

1229 For *chance* and mutability see *OK* 1080–86. For him Creon is but the occasion for traditional sententiousness.

1248 Cf. the riddling servant who flees Orestes:

> I tell you, he is alive and killing the dead.
>   (*Libation Bearers* 886)

Similarly, an ambiguity in 1250 leads to the question of 1252.

1262 *Pallas* is Athena.

1322–3 With her silence cf. *OK* 1076. Eurydice will not have been expected by the audience. Her silent departure, reminding us of Deianira (*Women of Trachis* 813), is ominous (*hope* usually deceives; see 667), and her suicide is calculated to enhance the grief and tragedy of Creon.

1338–9 *Ruin* (*atê*): see the notes on 666 and 1170. This traditional word for delusion/infatuation brought on by the gods has lost some of its precision but still has a bit of archaic awe in its wake. In 1339 there is an untranslated verb denoting his 'error' (see on 972).

1340 Here begins a lyric *kommos* (mourning song) which will take us to the end of the play.

1346 The language of this play has a more decided intellectual cast than most of Sophocles' plays. The word translated *folly* occurs elsewhere only in Antigone's 'my folly' (112); it is cognate with Teiresias' 'stupid' (1082) and messenger's 'wrong choice' (1320).

1347 For the motif *late* learning see 1422–4, *Women of Trachis* 708–11 and *Agamemnon* 176–8.

1349 *God*=a god; cf. 1418–19 and *OK* 1301. This is a commonplace metaphor for daimonic irruption in mental and moral purpose.

1361 For another metaphorical *haven* (harbor) see *OK* 1208.

1371 The *eccyclema* was a trolley pushed out onto the stage through the main door.

1379 *Megareus*: the allusion takes us to a prediction by Teiresias that only the death/sacrifice of a member of the royal family would save Thebes from the invading army (cf. 1123).

1394 *Guilt* is, in the usual rationalistic perspective of the play, 'responsibility' (cf. 'charge' at 489 and the use at 1248).

1398 *Best* has been 'profit', a characteristic point of view for Creon (240, 343, 1092–6, 1107).

1406–8 Yet Thebes is left with no male succession to the throne.

DAVID GRENE, Professor in the Committee on Social Thought at the University of Chicago, is the author of *Greek Political Theory: The Image of Man in Thucydides and Plato*. He is the translator of Herodotus' *History*, Aeschylus' *Prometheus Bound* and *Seven against Thebes*, Sophocles' *Electra* and *Philoctetes* and Euripides' *Hippolytus*, which are included in *The Complete Greek Tragedies*, published by the University of Chicago Press.

CHARLES SEGAL is Professor of Greek and Latin at Harvard University. His books include *Tragedy and Civilization: An Interpretation of Sophocles*, *Interpreting Greek Tragedy*, *Oedipus Tyrannus: Tragic Heroism and the Limits of Knowledge*, *Orpheus: The Myth of the Poet* and *Euripides and the Poetics of Sorrow*, with *Singers, Heroes and Gods in the Odyssey* forthcoming.

JAMES C. HOGAN is Frank T. McClure Professor of Classics at Allegheny College and author of *The Plays of Sophocles: A Companion to the University of Chicago Press Translations*.

RICHMOND LATTIMORE was Professor Emeritus of Greek at Bryn Mawr College at the time of his death in 1984. His many highly acclaimed translations of ancient Greek and Roman works include Homer's *Iliad* and the *Odes of Pindar*.